CHRISTIAN UNITY

IS VOLUME

138

OF THE

Twentieth Century Encyclopedia of Catholicism

UNDER SECTION

XIV

OUTSIDE THE CHURCH

IT IS ALSO THE

86TH

VOLUME IN ORDER OF PUBLICATION

Edited by HENRI DANIEL-ROPS of the Académie Française

CHRISTIAN UNITY

By *CHARLES BOYER, S.J.*

Translated from the Italian by JILL DEAN

HAWTHORN BOOKS · PUBLISHERS · *New York*

First Edition, May, 1962

NIHIL OBSTAT

Hubertus Richards, S.T.L., L.S.S.

   Censor Deputatus

IMPRIMATUR

E. Morrogh Bernard

   Vicarius Generalis

Westmonasterii, die II FEBRUARII, MCMLXII

CONTENTS

INTRODUCTION

THE PROBLEM OF CHRISTIAN UNITY

Christian unity is one of the crucial problems of our age, and the ecumenical movement one of the most important events which has arisen to combat the evil of disunion. Christians, if all those who recognize Jesus Christ as their Lord and their God are included in that term, are in fact profoundly divided, and today they suffer from their disunity more than ever. In the last fifty years, particularly, they have tried and continue to try to reunite what has become more and more broken up with the passing of the centuries. On one side are the Catholics who maintain that they have kept the essential unity since Christ, as they say, founded only one Church which must, therefore, be a united Church; it is of course open to all, but it includes only those who profess the same faith, are under the same government, and worship in the same way: for it is the Roman Church one, holy, catholic and apostolic. For these, the problems of Christian unity, to which they give intense and ever increasing attention, can be none other than the return of other Christians to the bosom of Catholic unity. On the other side, the separated brethren think that the visible unity which Christ desired no longer exists, and so they strive to restore it by various means, or at least they try to create an image as similar to it as possible.

The books and articles dealing with these problems constitute a formidable library. For the ever-growing public interested in Christian unity, the present work is intended to give an exact picture of the present situation and a survey of the ideas which should direct the work *pro unione.*

Although I do not conceal the fact that I write as a Catholic priest, I have endeavoured to maintain an objective view throughout. For this English edition I have revised the work and brought it up to date, as well as completing the bibliography.

CHAPTER I

THE PRESENT SITUATION

The ecumenical movement can be defined as the sum of all the attempts made from 1910 onwards to bring people together and to unite all the faithful of the different confessions. The etymological meaning of ecumenical is the same as "catholic" or universal; it is derived from the Greek *oikumeni,* which means the whole inhabited world. Its purpose, therefore, is to repair the divisions which have arisen throughout the centuries among those who believe in Christ. Without a knowledge of the present state of disunion of Christianity and without going back to the beginnings of the separations, it is impossible to understand the cause, the terms and the difficulties. At the outset we should recall the chief dates of the first divisions among Christians and then those at which they were continued or strengthened.

THE SEPARATED EASTERN CHURCHES

A very large number of Eastern Christians are not Catholics. They belong to what is called the Eastern Schism. It is difficult to know their exact number; some statistics put them at 144 million,[1] while others put them as high as 172 million.[2] In fact, to put it roughly, the number of non-Catholic Christians in the East is more than a third of the number of Catholics.

In the same way, it is difficult to give an exact date for the

[1] *World Almanac* (New York, 1934); Abbé D'Espierre (Braine-le-Comte, 1934), gives a few less: 143,625,297.

[2] Fr Janin in his book, *Les Eglises séparées d'Orient* (Paris, 1930), gave the figure 172,016,978.

beginning of the schism. For a long time, with Hefele[3] and Hergenrother,[4] it was said to have started with Photius, the patriarch of Constantinople, during the ninth century. Indeed, Photius, who twice ascended the patriarchal see of Constantinople and twice had to give it up, was certainly at variance with Rome during his patriarchate. Photius, an ordinary layman, was elected patriarch instead of the holy bishop Ignatius (858). Since the election gave rise to disputes, the Eastern people agreed that the great Pope Nicholas should intervene as judge. The papal legates confirmed the election of Photius (861) but Pope Nicholas did not accept this judgement and even sent some Latin missionaries to Bulgaria at the request of Boris, the king of the Bulgarians, and these supplanted the Greek missionaries there. Photius was angry, and wrote against the Latins, accusing them of many errors, and convoked a Council (867) by which he deposed Pope Nicholas. Shortly afterwards Photius himself was forced to abdicate. Ignatius returned, and a Council (the eighth) sanctioned these changes (869). But on the death of Ignatius, Photius re-ascended the patriarchal see, was reconciled with Pope John VIII at the price of a retraction, which he pronounced at a Council (878–80), which is called the Photian Council. From then on there was no more discord. The belief in a "second Photian schism" has definitely been destroyed in recent years.[5] He died in communion with the Byzantine Church, which was certainly united to Rome under Pope Stephen V (who died in 891) and John IX, who was elected in 898. Some think there was a schism under Pope Formosus (891–6). It is not known when Photius died.[6] All things considered, it must be concluded with Grumel that "in choosing a patron of unity Photius can be disregarded".

[3] *Histoire des Conciles.*

[4] *Photius,* III (Regensburg, 1867).

[5] V. Grumel in *Revue des Sciences Philosophiques,* 1933, pp. 432–57; and F. Dvornik, *The Photian Schism* (Cambridge, 1948); cf. V. Grumel, in *Unitas* (Italian ed. 1953), pp. 97–107.

[6] See Grumel, "Precisazioni sullo scisma di Fozio", in *Unitas* (new series), II (1953), pp. 97–107.

The present schism did not, therefore, start with Photius. Nevertheless, on account of the break which occurred during his patriarchate, and of his anti-Latin writings, he cannot be considered an apostle of unity.[7]

In fact, with Photius, the same pattern of relationships between Rome and Constantinople can be seen as before: discord, sometimes separation, and a real schism with reciprocal condemnations, all followed by a more or less difficult reconciliation. Arianism, Nestorianism, Monophysitism, Monothelitism and Iconoclasm are all names which recall impassioned conflicts between Rome and part, at least, of the East. Unity, always difficult to achieve among men, was certainly faced with special difficulties between East and West. On one side was Rome expressing herself in Latin, striving towards practical action, a lover of order and law and conscious of the primacy accorded her by her origin; for she had been founded by St Peter and yet she was ruled by barbarians. On the other side was Constantinople, home of the imperial court, with her Greek language, her great doctors, her taste for ideas and debates, her court intrigues, and her feeling for a more ancient and more cultured civilization. Good relations between the two capitals were certainly still possible, but there were real difficulties, especially when political interests clashed.

The differences between East and West had gradually increased: different languages, different customs, even in Christian practice, such as fasting and the administration of the sacraments. There were also some differences of doctrine which arose from time to time after the innovations of Photius. Add to these difficulties the effects of nationalism, and the difficulty in which the patriarch of the imperial city found himself of giving up first place to a bishop from the barbarous West, and it will be easy to understand how, after numerous disagreements and various separations, more or less hastily repaired, a lasting schism came into existence, as soon as an ambitious patriarch appeared who desired and organized it.

[7] Cf. F. Dvornik, "Photius père du schisme ou apôtre de l'union?" in *La vie intellectuelle*, December 1945, pp. 16–28.

For over a century after Photius, unity was preserved. At the beginning of the eleventh century, relations became very strained because of the dissension which had arisen between the Latin emperor, the pope's ally, and the Byzantine emperors.

The last pope whose name is to be found in the diptychs of Constantinople is John XVIII, who died in 1009. This state of tension was not yet a break. Various attempts at forming an alliance were made between Pope Leo IX and the Emperor Constantine IX for a common line of defence against the Normans. But the patriarch, Michael Cerularius, not only wanted to treat the Roman See as an equal, but ascribed to himself a primacy of orthodoxy. He insisted that before any agreement, the Latins must renounce a great many of their customs which he called errors. Michael attacked the Latin Church on the question of the azymes: for the Latins consecrate the Eucharist with unleavened bread, while the Greeks use leavened bread. He closed the Latin churches in Constantinople and refused to discuss the question with the papal legates who had been sent to the patriarchal city for that purpose.

The papal legate, Cardinal Umberto, tried in vain to put things right and, when he failed to do so, excommunicated Cerularius (in fact the excommunication was legally null because it took place after the death of the pope, but it was confirmed later) and placed the Bull on the altar of St Sophia on July 16th, 1054. Cerularius excommunicated the legates. This was schism. Probably at the time everybody thought it would be of short duration like so many others, but in fact it is the one which persists today.

However, there have been many attempts at reunion.[8] Also in the eleventh century a council was held at Bari (1038), at which St Anselm was present. Various conversations took place between the Greeks and Latins at Constantinople during the following century. But political tension between the Latins and the Greeks, and the behaviour of the Crusaders towards

[8] Cf. G. Hoffmann, S.J., "I Papi del Medio Evo e l'unione delle Chiese orientali con la Chiesa cattolica", in *Incontro ai fratelli separati di Oriente* (Rome, U.M.C., 1945), pp. 155–64, with good bibliography.

the Byzantine Empire, widened the abyss of separation. When
the Crusaders were driven out of Constantinople, the victor,
Michael Paleologus, thought about reuniting Christians. The
negotiations started under Urban IV who asked St Thomas
Aquinas to make a study of the Greek errors, and sent a repre-
sentative to the Emperor. His successor, Clement IV, sent a
profession of faith to Paleologus, which he accepted. Then the
question came before the Council of Lyons in 1274, called together by Gregory X. The Greek representatives accepted the
profession of faith required by Clement IV, and Gregory
celebrated the reunion with a solemn pontifical Mass in the
cathedral of Lyons, at which St Bonaventure preached the sermon. A week later, when the formalities had been completed,
the pope solemnly proclaimed the union of the Churches. However, it did not last even ten years. Already in 1282, Androni-
kos Paleologus, the son of Michael, tried to break it. About
fifty years later, the Turkish danger made the Greeks think of
reunion. Various steps were taken on both sides, including the
reconciliation of the Emperor John V.

In the fifteenth century, at the request of the Byzantine
Emperor John VII Paleologus, Martin V decided to convoke
a council for reunion. His successor, Eugenius IV, and the
Council of Basle were in agreement about holding the council,
but not on where it should take place. The pope prevailed and
the council was convoked at Ferrara, but as it soon moved to
Florence, it is known by that city's name.

Many Eastern delegates came to Ferrara and Florence.
There were about 700 Byzantines and some Russians. The
pope paid for their maintenance and also for their journey.
The patriarchs of Constantinople, Antioch and Jerusalem and
Alexandria were represented; and so were the metropolitans
of Turkish Asia Minor, Bulgaria and Russia. There were also
monks and priests belonging to the lower clergy. The Greeks
were at liberty to expound their opinions. Agreement was
reached, largely due to the efforts of Bessarion for the Easterns,
and the Dominican John Torquemada for the Latins. On July
6th, 1439, the reunion of the Greek Church was proclaimed in

the cathedral of Florence, and a plaque was placed in the apse to commemorate the event.

But even now agreement was not maintained. One of the delegates to Florence, Mark of Ephesus, who was opposed to reunion, conducted a vigorous campaign against it; at his instigation the lower clergy and the monks urged the people to resist, and the higher clergy followed. The reunion was only proclaimed in Constantinople on December 12th, 1452; but five months later the Turks occupied the city. However, both before and after this disaster, the Eastern hierarchy violently rejected the Council of Florence and its decrees. From then on the schism has endured.

The historian should not consider that the efforts of the two councils were in vain, because the possibility of agreement on dogmatic questions was established. Important doctrinal documents were drawn up there in a spirit of peace. Also the obstacles which ought to be avoided in any new attempt were made clear: the unpreparedness of the people who did not understand the action of their leaders, the interference of politics, and especially the memory of the very recent outrages perpetrated by the Latins in the East.

When separation or schism occurs in a religious society, it is usually accompanied by differences of doctrine. In fact the very rejection of the real supremacy of the Roman pope constituted a true heresy to Catholic eyes. The Ecumenical Council of Florence, and more clearly still the Vatican Council, have defined that the bishop of Rome is the successor of Peter and supreme head of the Church, and have declared that all Christians owe him obedience. Furthermore, those who break away appeal to doctrinal differences to justify their actions, and these differences, with the passing of time, tend to increase and become more serious. Let us consider the doctrinal differences between the Eastern and Western Christians at the present time.

The most important difference is rather subtle, and not very well understood, except by theologians. The Latins, already with Tertullian and St Hilary, and especially with St Augustine, define the mystery of the Trinity by saying that the Third Person, the Holy Spirit, proceeds from the other two; that is, not only from the Father, but also from the Son. Thus they interpret the Gospel of St John, in which it is written that the Son communicates his own knowledge to the Spirit and sends him to his disciples, which means that the Son operates as generator towards the Spirit, which in the Supreme Being cannot be other than by direct and complete communication of the one and only divine nature. Further, if the Son, as he affirms, possesses all that the Father possesses, he must also have the generating action of the Holy Spirit. The Greeks, on the other hand, following Photius in this matter, maintain that the Holy Spirit proceeds only from the Father.

The fact that some "orthodox" theologians have said that it is only a matter of opinion, and not of dogma, does not help much, because the Catholic Church defined her position at Florence, and she sings it in the creed of Nicaea-Constantinople: *Qui a Patre Filioque procedit*. It is true that the *Filioque* was added in the seventh century in Spain, but the Latins hold that this was not a change but merely a more exact definition of a belief already professed, which they thought opportune to define.

It should be explained at once that there are two formulas on this subject, which could promote agreement. One is that used by the Eastern Fathers, Origen, St Basil and St Cyril of Alexandria, which says that the Spirit proceeds from the Father through the Son (διὰ τοῦ Υἱου) and which was accepted by Pope Adrian as equivalent to the Latin one; and in fact it seems to be so. The other is a Latin formula, from St Augustine, and says that the Spirit proceeds from the Father and from the Son, but chiefly from the Father, *principaliter a Patre,* because the Son receives his generating act of the Holy Spirit from the Father: thus the Father keeps his character of first principle in the Trinity, on which the Greeks are so insistent.[9]

[9] *De Trinitate*, Bk. 15, ch. 17, n. 29. See Volume 17 in this series, pp. 120 following.

However history shows that the doctrinal differences between East and West are the effect rather than the cause of the schism. Submission to the bishop of Rome had become hateful. If that were to become welcome again, all the differences of faith would also disappear.

Therefore, it is easy to understand that the duration of the schism for so many centuries could not but widen the abyss between the two Churches. The events of history hardened hearts on both sides. The Crusaders crossed the Byzantine Empire, bringing with them the outrages and damage common to every army on the march, the more severe in this case owing to lack of discipline. The fourth crusade was particularly ruinous, for it even sacked Constantinople. Also some ecclesiastics made the mistake of wanting to impose the Latin liturgy on the Greeks. Thus, the hatred of Rome and the Latins was fostered by the sins and mistakes of men. The isolation inflicted by the Turkish domination completed the separation and nourished bitterness.

Another theoretical and practical difference developed at the same time, which is a grave obstacle to reconciliation, namely the different attitude towards divorce. While Rome does not allow it in any case, the Greeks grant it very easily. The Greeks appeal to the text of St Matthew: "And I tell you that he who puts away his wife, except for any unfaithfulness of hers, and so marries another, commits adultery",[10] and conclude that there is an exception to indissolubility, the case of fornication, that is adultery. In practice, though, many other cases are made an exception.[11] The Catholics explain those verses of St Matthew differently. They refer to the text of St Mark which says, "If a man puts away his wife and marries another, he behaves adulterously towards her"[12] and to the words of St Paul about married women, "She will be held an adultress if she gives herself to another man during her hus-

---

[10] Matthew 19. 9.
[11] See M. Jugie, in *Unitas*, I (1946), pp. 43-61.
[12] Mark 10. 11. See also Luke 16. 18.

band's lifetime".[13] Therefore, they do not recognize any exceptions.

Political events explain how the schism, which started in Constantinople, spread all over the East. Russia was on the Greek side because it had been evangelized before the schism by Byzantine missionaries. There was no act of separation for Russia, because it was in the Byzantine communion and did not deal with Rome, but it was in fact a separation. It was only later, chiefly in the nineteenth century, that it showed opposition and hatred towards the Roman Church. It was more or less the same in Bulgaria, Serbia and Georgia, which were separated from Rome without any action of their own, but with the passing of time, that separation in fact became an accepted and declared schism.

We can turn now to the present situation. The separated Eastern Churches call themselves "Orthodox" to show that they have kept the purity of the faith.[14] They are autocephalous, that is each one is independent. An honorary primacy is conceded to the patriarch of Constantinople, but today it seems as though the patriarch of Moscow exercises a more real primacy. Supreme power ought to belong to the Ecumenical Council, but that is not possible, say the Orthodox, while the schism continues so that, since 787, the date of the Seventh Council, it has not been possible to make any infallible decisions. The different dissident Churches are, first and foremost, that of Constantinople, then those of the patriarchs of Alexandria, Antioch and Jerusalem; then there are the ancient Churches of Cyprus and Sinai, and those which have separated from the patriarchate of Constantinople, namely, the Russian Church, the patriarch of which lives in Moscow, the Bulgarian Church, the Serbian Church, the Rumanian Church and the Greek Church. After the first world war, other Churches declared themselves independent in the Baltic States, in Poland, in Czechoslovakia, in Albania, in North America and Japan.

[13] Romans 7. 2.
[14] Before the schism, the expression "Orthodox Church" was used for both the Eastern and Western Churches.

Emigrations brought about by the Russian revolution have divided them further still in the European capitals, and the two Americas.

The Greeks, too, did not consider the separation of the eleventh century permanent and definitive. Many meetings and isolated acts of reunion took place until the fall of Constantinople. The isolation caused by Turkish rule made the separation worse, and later, especially from the nineteenth century until today, it became openly hostile. The establishment of so many independent autocephalous Churches naturally favours differences of discipline and even of faith. Even in the same Church, political events lead to serious differences. The metropolitan Anastasias, who opposes the patriarch Alexei of Moscow, is recognized by many Russian emigrants in France, Belgium, Switzerland, England and Italy. There may even be clandestine opposition in Russia.

In the East there are also Christians whose separation is older. They are what remains of the heresies of the fourth and fifth centuries, the Monophysites, half of which are to be found in Ethiopia, and others in Armenia and with the Copts in Antioch and Jerusalem, who, with Eutyches, believe that there is only one nature in Christ. It is estimated that their number does not exceed eight million. The Nestorians, that is those who with Nestorius believe that there are two persons in Christ, the divine person and the human person, are less numerous, possibly only 85,000, and they are to be found in Iraq, Iran and possibly elsewhere.

But not all Christians in the East are schismatic. At the end of the Second World War, the Catholic Church still had nine million members there, belonging to communities which throughout the centuries have preserved unity or have returned to it. This Catholic minority has been officially rejected with violence by the schismatic Russians; but it should be remembered that many consciences may have remained faithful to Roman unity. The Maronites of the Lebanon have never been separated. The Ruthenians, whose Church was flourishing until recently, are at present suffering a relentless persecution from the Communists. Among the Rumanians, Melkites, Bulgarians, Greeks, Albanians, Copts, Armenians, Syrians and Chaldeans, there are isolated groups of Catholics who keep their own language, liturgy and rite, and thus pave the way to unity for the dissident.

PROTESTANTISM

Meanwhile another serious separation had occurred, which separated half the West from Rome. When historians describe the state of the Church at the beginning of the sixteenth century, they cannot of course say that the Lutheran revolt was inevitable, but they can show fairly well how it was possible for it to happen, and to have such enormous success.

Martin Luther was indeed the principal author of it, but many other people and many other reasons caused the monk's action to have such a great and lasting effect. The existence in the Church of many abuses and many disorders, the egoism of the sovereigns who were eager to obtain independence and greedily desired to take possession of ecclesiastical property, the awakening of nationalism, the weakening of faith brought about by the Renaissance, the decadence of the scholastic system: all these events together made the atmosphere favourable to the Lutheran revolution and to the recruitment of his followers. These, too, had a strong influence on Luther himself.

On all sides there was a call to reform the abuses, which were grave and continuous. At other times, in similar circumstances, reform had been directed from within, but since Luther soon rebelled against the pope, he was forced to try to do it from without. The truth is, that when he started his movement by affixing his ninety-five theses to the doors of the University of Wittenberg, a theology had already developed which was radically opposed to Catholic theology. The decisive event, which had been able to arouse religious enthusiasm immediately and was later to form the basis of Protestantism, had occurred a few years before the open revolt. Luther had lived the first years of his religious life esteemed by his superiors and in regular observance, but his soul was tormented by an obsession with sin and by the violence of temptations. He was oppressed by the feeling of an inclination towards evil; justification and sanctity seemed to him to be inaccessible. As he tells us later, it was not by any sudden light, but by slow steps,[15] that by reading St Paul he became convinced that the goodness that saves us is not our own, but that of God himself which is attributed to us through the merits of Christ. We are sinners, and we remain sinners; but God regards those who believe as though they were just.

Man cannot help being a sinner, always a sinner; so he is never just through his own justice, but God looks at the justice of Christ and, because of this justice, he forgives the sins of those who want to believe in that forgiveness. Luther thought that faith alone was sufficient, as the Scripture, which is the only authority, promises. Therefore good works have no merit; the sacraments, of which there are only two or three (Baptism, the Eucharist and to a certain extent Penance) serve only to arouse faith; the priesthood consists only of preaching, which all can do; the Church can do nothing for those who have no faith; reason is impotent in the moral and religious sphere; the liberty of God abolishes that of man; the Bible is the sole criterion of truth. Thus, the hierarchy, the authority of the pope, the priesthood, the Mass and the sacraments are dethroned, and the arbitrary will of God and private judgement are established. Luther did not at first foresee all these consequences, but they followed from the principles held by him. Once he had committed himself, Luther conducted the battle with all the fire and fury of his powerful nature. It was then that all the general causes, operative throughout the Christian community, came into play and gave to the theological controversy sufficient strength to divide the believers of Europe in two. The German princes found in the reform occasion to satisfy their temporal interests. As is well known the greater part of Germany, also through the efforts of the princes, followed the new doctrine, and was thus separated from Rome. The movement

---

[15] See the Waldensian G. Miegge's *Lutero* ("Luther"), ɪ (Torre Pellice, Claudiana, 1946), pp. 29 ff.

did not stop at the Rhine, but spread, either immediately or later, to Switzerland, France, Scandinavia and England, and from thence to America.

In Switzerland, Ulrich Zwingli, a devoted admirer of Erasmus, echoed the appeal of Luther to the Gospel alone against the authority of the pope and won Zurich and twelve other cantons to his views, so that when he was killed, at the battle of Cappel in 1531, he left Switzerland prepared for Calvin's work. It was Calvin who started the Reformation, probably in 1533, and was extraordinarily successful. He not only dominated Geneva, moulding the city according to his own ideas, but managed to draw up such a clear and complete theological system that it became the accepted code of a great number of Protestants, for those in Switzerland, Holland and France are predominantly Calvinists and in Great Britain and America they form an important minority.

Sweden, Norway and Denmark were dragged into Lutheranism against the wishes of the people by their sovereigns, Gustavus Vasa and Christian III. The Netherlands took the opportunity of getting rid of the Hapsburgs. Likewise England renounced obedience to the pope through her king, Henry VIII, and gradually changed from a state of schism to the essential doctrines of Calvinism, through the efforts of Cranmer. The colonization of America and the expansion of the British Empire have spread Anglicanism and the Protestant sects to other parts of the world.

From the start, there was some Lutheran infiltration into France. The anti-Catholic movement was greatly reinforced by the action of Calvin. The Protestants became so strong that they were able to resist the royal power with arms. Civil war and massacres lasted until the reign of Henry IV, who became a Catholic (1593). From that time on Protestants have been a small but not uninfluential minority in France.

Thus a great part of Europe gave up obedience to the pope and Catholic orthodoxy. The consequences of this are abundantly evident today.

In Germany, Holland and America, the Catholics, although a minority, are numerous and active. But there are very few in Scandinavia, in spite of the recent creation of the bishoprics of Copenhagen and Stockholm. In England, where the hierarchy has been re-established, Catholicism is lively and active, but there are not yet five million Catholics.

When considering the dissident Oriental Churches, a doctrine more or less common to all can be seen, but that is not the case when considering the followers of the Reformation. At the very beginning, and even at the time of Luther, there arose many differences of doctrine, and the leaders of the movement fought bitterly among themselves.

A century later, Bossuet wrote the history of the Protestant differences; and although he may have had too narrow a concept of the essential immutability of doctrine, he nevertheless ably demonstrated the important and irreconcilable conflicts amongst the reformers which had already arisen in his time. The disunity has continued.

It is not within our scope to enumerate the different sects. It is sufficient for us to distinguish four principal groups: the Anglicans, the Lutherans, the Calvinists and the Nonconformists.

The Anglicans, members of the established (State) Church of England and the Episcopalians of America, have episcopal government. They recognize a certain honorary primacy in the Archbishop of Canterbury. These are said to be High or Low Church, according to the degree of positivity and complexity of their doctrines and worship. Prominent amongst those who are High Church are the Anglo-Catholics, who are closest to the Roman Catholic Church. Four points of doctrine were declared essential for Anglicanism at the Lambeth Conference in 1888, and these are: the Bible, as rule and ultimate standard of faith; the Nicene Creed, as sufficient statement of the Christian faith; the sacraments of Baptism and Holy Communion, as the expression of charity in Christ; a ministry which has received from Christ authority over the whole body. These four points are known as the Lambeth Quadrilateral.

The Nonconformists, who are numerous in England and America, separated from the Anglican Church, because they wanted greater liberty, or, also, more religious fervour. They formed the various communions, as, for example, the Presbyterians, the Baptists, the Congregationalists, the Methodists, the Quakers, etc.

Liberalism and modernism became widespread among Protestants in the nineteenth century and at the beginning of the twentieth. But a reaction, due largely to the Calvinist, Karl Barth, has brought many of them back to belief in the principal Christian dogmas.

THE UNHAPPY EFFECTS OF SEPARATION

We must endeavour to understand the tragic consequences of the disunity of Christians. First and foremost such disunity of Christians is contrary to the expressed will of Jesus Christ, so every Christian should deplore it. It is with reason that the Protestants, the Anglicans and the Orthodox have recognized the confusion in which they find themselves as a result of their loss of unity, and they have attributed it to the sins of men. At Evanston this was stated openly.[16]

In fact, our Saviour prayed to the Father after the Last Supper, and asked above all for the unity of his Church: "Holy Father," he said for his apostles, "keep them true to thy name, thy gift to me, that they may be one, as we are one."[17] And then, speaking for all the faithful: :"It is not only for them that I pray; I pray for those who are to find faith in me through their word; that they may all be one; that they too may be one in us, as thou Father, art in me, and I in thee; so that the world may come to believe that it is thou who hast sent me. And I have given them the privilege which thou gavest to me, that they should all be one, as we are one; that while thou art in me, I may be in them, and so they may be perfectly made one. So let the world know that it is thou who hast sent me, and

---

[16] See Section 1, *Faith and Order*, n. 15.
[17] John 17. 11.

that thou hast bestowed thy love upon them, as thou hast bestowed it upon me." [18]

No Christian, whether a Catholic or not, can deny that Christ expressed in that great prayer his desire that his own should be one. He who wants to be of Christ should love and seek and keep that unity. Catholics believe that such a prayer could not remain unanswered, and that these words refer to themselves, since they are united in the same faith, under the same head, in the same worship, however different they may be in every other way. This explains the desire which urges them to communicate their unity to all those who bear the name of Christians.

All Christians, who are praying and working for Christian unity, must react against confusion, and notice how much has been done against Christ's will.

This disunity is largely responsible for the enormous number of non-Christians still living on the whole face of the earth. In the countries of the West, the religious wars, the bitter discussions and quarrels among the different influences and other consequences of the Reformation, have certainly helped to increase the number of sceptics and of the indifferent, and to diminish the power of the Church. It is certainly true that some well-known Protestants, such as Ribot, have defended Christian causes which benefited Catholics above all; but alas, how often have our quarrels helped our common enemies! In the East, the Churches have closed in on themselves, and, until today, have lost the spirit of conquest. Being too closely linked with the civil powers, they have suffered from the consequences of revolutions and have hardly put up any resistance to the onslaught of atheism. If only all those who are followers of Christ had formed a solid block, held together and directed by one hierarchy, the widespread apostasies, which have occurred ever since the eighteenth century, would not have taken place, and a great many other disasters which have clouded recent history could certainly have been avoided.

[18] John 17. 20–3.

But it is above all in the missionary countries that the evil caused by disunity is so noticeable. For a long time the task of evangelization had been left to the Catholic Church alone. Later the Protestant missions were established, and these have, it is true, shown a true sense of religion and a praiseworthy spirit of sacrifice; but it is a matter for regret for Christians that so much effort has been expended by scattered groups, often opposed to one another. If it had been done with the cohesion and enthusiasm of a single organization, perhaps the whole world would be Christian today. The very fact that those believers who go to convert the pagans are divided in their own faith causes the testimony of the missionaries to lose its clarity and much of its strength. When it is recalled that in China more than sixty Christian sects have propagated the faith, there will be less surprise that the number of Christians there is still so small. And what is true of China is true of Japan and India. It was because they were aware of the obstacle set up by their disunity that the Protestant missionaries organized a Congress at Edinburgh in 1910 to consider the possibilities and means to unity; and it was that Congress which inspired Charles Brent with the idea of the Ecumenical Movement. Supposing there had been no schism, and that first Europe and later America had sent missionaries to preach the same faith to the rest of the world, with at least all the resources that have been gathered together for the missions, would there be upwards of a thousand million non-Christians left on the earth today?

In Leo XIII's letter *Praeclara*, in which he invited all Christians to unite, he said: "Most certainly, the counsels of God with regard to the eternal salvation of peoples are far removed above the understanding of man; yet if miserable superstition still prevails in so many parts of the world, the blame must be attributed in no small measure to religious dissensions."

The Protestant theologian, Karl Barth, has written: "In the missions, where Christianity is confronted with pagan religions, where is the Church? There is not one: there are many who quarrel amongst themselves. And so what a weakening of spiritual and even material strength of the missions! How can the message be heard? How tedious for the superficial listener! How bewildering for the serious listener!"[19] Some decades ago the review *Irenikon* quoted these words from a Buddhist newspaper.

> The Christian missionaries in India, in China and in Japan have made a fatal error by trying to convert some to the Anglican Church, some Americans to Presbyterianism or else to German Lutheranism. They forgot that these different forms of Christianity grew up out of the needs of special and local circumstances. That is why they fail so miserably. They do not know how to present the spirit of Christianity.[20]

Fr Jean Daniélou says: "I never think without sorrow of the spectacle which those divided Churches, calling themselves Christians and yet opposed to one another, offer to the pagans. What a cry of indignation those Christians, who set up rivalry between the Churches within the community, called forth from St Paul, 'Is Christ then divided?' Where Christ is, can there be divisions? And if there is division, is Christ still there?"[21]

At the Ecumenical Assemblies, those who are called the "young Churches", that is the Protestant African or Asiatic communities, appear to be impatient of the divisions they have inherited.

At the spectacle of the modern progress of irreligion and atheism, it is to be wished that all those who are in the service of God's cause should form one body to confront the attack, and regain positions which have been lost. Unfortunately, the state of disunion cannot but lessen their strength and enthusiasm. It is not sufficient, in order to fight together, to be in agreement on a few fundamental truths, when there is disagreement on others of no less importance, which are necessarily almost always connected. Mutual trust is not complete, interests do not coincide and work is uncoordinated, so therefore hindered. Thus there is only one remedy, reunion.

---

[19] In *Oecumenica*, July 1943, p. 137.
[20] *Irenikon*, 1927, p. 479.
[21] *Dialogues*, 1948, p. 125.

Speaking at Malines of the primacy (insufficient from the Catholic point of view) which he himself and his friends were ready to accord to the Roman Pontiff, Dr B. J. Kidd declared that they had been led to it by "our feeling of the urgent necessity for the ranks of Christians to unite within the Church, to face the chaotic condition of things, and to stand up to the forces of evil from without".[22]

[22] J. de Bivort de la Saudée, *Documents sur le problème de l'union anglo-romaine* (1921–1927), (Paris, 1949), p. 172.

CHAPTER II

THE ECUMENICAL MOVEMENT

Protestants found a special reason in their own internal disunity for wanting union. But, also, attempts at reunion with the Catholic Church occurred from the beginning of the Reformation. In fact it could be said that separation was not Luther's intention at first. His closest disciple, Melanchthon, tried to effect a reconciliation. Afterwards hope was placed in a council. Then, when all means had failed, many generous souls refused to accept it as a definite break, and tried hard to put it right.

Particularly remarkable were the attempts made by Bossuet and Leibniz. In *A History of the Ecumenical Movement* published recently,[1] more than 350 pages are devoted to a description of the various attempts at reunion amongst Christians; but, in most cases, it is only dealing with partial approaches, in which the Roman Catholic Church was rarely concerned.

An Anglican clergyman, the Revd Spencer Jones, who tried to lead England to reconciliation with the See of Peter, wanted the feast of St Peter to be observed by sermons on the Petrine prerogatives. A friend of his, the Revd Paul Watson, an Episcopalian, suggested that it would be better to choose the Octave beginning with the feast of St Peter's Chair, on January 18th, and ending with the feast of the Conversion of St Paul on January 25th. But very soon Watson became a Catholic, to-

[1] Ruth Rouse and S. C. Neill, *A History of the Ecumenical Movement, 1517–1948* (London, S.P.C.K., 1954).

gether with the two Congregations which he had founded (Brothers and Sisters of the Atonement), and in December, 1909, St Pius X gave his blessing to the celebration of the Octave. It is precisely in 1910 that the Ecumenical Movement started. We can repeat the words of the historians of the movement: "The whole story should teach us something of the way in which God moves the world through the Church by leading his faithful people to pray for those things which it is his will to grant" (op. cit., p. 349).

The missionaries, belonging to the various communions derived from the Reformation, held a Congress at Edinburgh in 1910 for the purpose of uniting among themselves as closely as possible. Charles Brent, who was then the Episcopalian bishop of the Philippines, was present, and it was his idea to extend the efforts for unity to include all Christians.

The Congress had given him a vision of a united Church and he said: "Whenever God gives us a vision he also points to some new responsibility, and you and I, when we leave this assembly, will go away with fresh duties to perform".[2] The following motion was unanimously accepted: "That a joint commission be appointed to bring about a conference for the consideration of questions touching Faith and Order, and that all Christian Communions throughout the world which confess our Lord Jesus Christ as God and Saviour be asked to unite with us in arranging for the conducting of such a conference."[3] A layman, Robert Gardiner, was elected Secretary of the Commission, and he was mainly responsible for the work. The movement spread rapidly. J. Pierpoint Morgan at once gave a donation of 100,000 dollars. Letters and deputations were sent everywhere, preparatory meetings were held and commissions set up. A meeting of fifteen commissions took place in New York in 1913. Here are two of their conclusions, which explain the movement:

1. That the true ideal of the World Conference is of a great meeting participated in by men of all Christian Churches within

[2] Quoted op. cit., p. 407.
[3] Ibid, p. 413.

the scope of the call, at which there shall be consideration not only of points of difference and agreement between Christians, but of the values of the various approximations to belief characteristic of the several Churches.

2. That while organic unity is the ideal which all Christians should have in their thoughts and prayers, yet the business of the Commissions is not to force any particular scheme of unity, but to promote the holding of such a Conference as is above described.[4]

In 1914, Gardiner wrote to Cardinal Gasparri, the Secretary of State, to inform him of the projected conference. He received a very courteous reply which concluded by saying that the pope was praying for the success of the venture, particularly because "with the voice of Christ himself sounding before and bidding him, he knows that he himself . . . is the source and cause of the unity of the Church".[5]

The First World War interrupted the carrying-out of the project. When hostilities were over, a deputation arrived in Rome, in 1919, to invite the Catholic Church to the Conference. Benedict XV received the delegates with great kindness, but he declined the invitation, with vigour. As they left the audience, a written statement was handed to them:

The Holy Father, after having thanked them for their visit, stated that as successor of St Peter and Vicar of Christ he had no greater desire than that there should be one fold and one shepherd. His Holiness added that the teaching and practice of the Roman Catholic Church regarding the unity of the visible Church of Christ was well known to everybody and therefore it would not be possible for the Catholic Church to take part in such a congress as the one proposed. His Holiness, however, by no means wishes to disapprove of the Congress in question for those who are not in union with the Chair of Peter, on the contrary, he earnestly desires and prays that, if the Congress is practicable, those who take part in it may, by the grace of God, see the light and become reunited to the visible Head of the Church, by whom they will be received with open arms.[6]

[4] Quoted in Rouse and Neill, *op. cit.*, p. 411.
[5] *Ibid.*, p. 413.
[6] Quoted *op. cit.*, p. 416.

The Christian communities, whose doctrines did not dissuade but rather urged them to look for what was missing, *Una Sancta*, the only Church founded by Christ, eagerly joined in with the intentions of those who were praying for unity. Various conferences were held, but very soon two currents appeared: one, which was more concerned with an understanding about action than with agreement about doctrine, was called "Work and Life", the other which paid more attention to doctrinal needs, was called "Faith and Order". The first was directed by the Lutheran bishop of Upsala, Nathan Söderblom; the second was under the influence of Charles Brent, who had become bishop of New York. In 1919, Söderblom held a preparatory meeting at The Hague, but in 1925 his group met again for an important conference at Stockholm, which lasted from August 19th–29th, and assembled 610 delegates from thirty-one different communions. According to the spirit of the Work and Life group, agreement was reached on practical action. In particular, a Christian social programme was established which, in fact, is very similar to the programmes drawn up in the Catholic Social Weeks.

In fact, it is easier to reach agreement between Catholics and other Christians on social questions.[7] But in spite of the emphasis on practical problems, the members of the Congress of Stockholm were aware of and troubled by their doctrinal differences. But the uneasiness was felt still more by the other movement, Faith and Order, when it held its conference at Lausanne in 1927, under the presidency of Charles Brent. The Eastern Orthodox, especially, dwelt much on the differences which separated them from the Protestants. In spite of this, the two movements could not keep apart, and in fact, although they planned another separate conference, they chose the same year and two cities which were quite close together. In 1937, therefore, the pragmatist group (Work and Life) met at Oxford, and the other doctrinal group at Edinburgh. The members of the Congress at Oxford realized that action is inseparable from

[7] This has been particularly remarked by the Protestant A. Keller. Cf. *Christian Europe Today* (New York and London, 1942), p. 255.

doctrine, and both groups laid open the way to unity. Seven delegates from each section were chosen, and they met in London to prepare a meeting to be held in 1939 at Utrecht. This meeting was presided over by the Anglican Archbishop of York, William Temple, who afterwards became archbishop of Canterbury. They decided on the establishment of a "Universal (or Ecumenical) Council of Churches", and a provisional committee took on the task of organizing the General Assembly of all the adherents of the Council. The Assembly was first forecast for 1941, but was postponed because of the war, and eventually took place in 1948 at Amsterdam.

This meeting, which a long and rather turbulent history had prepared, was of great importance. It was composed of the delegates of 148 denominations, including those of Ethiopia, India and Japan. The vast majority belonged to the various forms of Protestantism, while the separated Eastern brethren were scarcely represented, but to make up for that, they had sent important figures, such as the Greek Bishop Germanos and Professor Florovsky. The Synod of Moscow refused to participate, saying that the Assembly was not sufficiently democratic. The Catholic Church maintained the position taken up by Benedict XV; she followed this meeting of Christians with prayers and good wishes, but no Catholic was present either as a delegate or as an observer, either official or otherwise. This was a long way from Charles Brent's dream of forty years previously, of getting together an assembly of delegates of every group bearing the name of Christ; nevertheless, it was an occurrence of considerable importance, and it could only result in some consequences for the development of unionist movements.

The delegates of Amsterdam were acutely aware of the stumbling-block of their deep differences. It is all very well to emphasize the need for the spirit of understanding, of "comprehensiveness": doctrinal opposition cannot be overcome when it reaches a certain gravity and touches the conscience. Whoever believes that Jesus Christ promised us his real presence, body and soul, in the Eucharist, cannot feel in communion of faith with those who regard the bread of the Last Supper as a mere symbol. It is not only that they cannot celebrate the Eucharist together, but they would suffer such want of harmony as to feel themselves indeed separated brethren. The same thing happens on the questions of recognizing one authority in the Church whether it be an authority of order or of jurisdiction, of admitting the sacraments or not and of the cultus of the Blessed Virgin (whether it is regarded as idolatry or encouraged).

Precisely these differences, together with others, existed in this Assembly whose object was a display of unity. Of course we recognize that the quest for unity, shown to the world with such an imposing effort, and accompanied by sincere prayer, does constitute a certain progress, and bears within it the promise of better things to come; but that does not allow us to exaggerate the actual degree of unity which was achieved at Amsterdam. The words spoken by Karl Barth, whether in unofficial discussion, or at the public sessions held in the Concertgebouw Hall, show not only a real aversion towards the Roman Church, but also the impossibility of real understanding amongst the members of the Ecumenical Council.[8] In fact, Barth rebuked Rome for two things: the cult of the Mother of God, and the intransigence with which the Catholic Church proclaims herself the Church of Christ. The cult of Mary is held in great honour by the Eastern Christians who were present at the Congress of Amsterdam, and also among some Anglicans. And, if it is judged unacceptable that one Church claims to be that which Christ founded, the ecumenical movement, the object of which was to form such a Church, loses its justification, and deteriorates into universal and final relativism. Catholics cannot understand how Karl Barth who fought meritoriously and efficaciously against liberalism, and to restore among the Protestants

[8] By Ecumenical Council is usually meant a general Council of the Church, such as the Vatican Council, the Council of Trent or the first Council of the Lateran. Here the term is applied by the author to the meetings of the World Council of Churches, but there is no intention of equating the two meanings as is obvious from the context.—*Editor*.

the idea of dogma, does not see that, firstly, to accept inter-
mediaries such as Mary and the priesthood between God and
ourselves means to introduce not obstacles, but helps, and that,
secondly, our Redeemer could not have failed in his purpose
and founded a Church which after twenty centuries is still not
to be found anywhere.

CHAPTER III

FROM 1948 TO THE PRESENT

AFTER AMSTERDAM

At the great Conference the World Council of Churches had been established with a complex, precise organization.

The Council itself is the union of those "Churches" which have given it their assent, by accepting its basis and programme. In August 1954, there were 163 "Churches, i.e. groups with a certain amount of independence, distinguished either by different confessions of faith, or by minor differences of nationality, place, language, etc." The Council is conducted by six presidents, chosen from among the different confessions. The following were chosen at Evanston to govern the Council until the next Assembly in 1960: Otto Dibelius, the Evangelical bishop of Berlin and president of the German Evangelist Church; Knox Sherrie, of New York, bishop and president of the Protestant Episcopalian Church of the United States; Juhanon Mar Thoma, metropolitan of the Syrian Church of Malabar; John Baillie, of the Scottish Church, principal of New College at the University of Edinburgh; Michael, Orthodox archbishop for the two Americas; Sante Barbieri, Methodist bishop for the Argentine, Uruguay and Bolivia.

Supreme authority, however, belongs to the Assembly, composed of the official representatives of all the member Churches, which meets every five years. In the meantime, the management belongs to a Central Committee, composed of the six presidents and the ninety elected members.

The Council then entrusts some of its duties to Commissions, the most important of which continues the Faith and Order movement.

The President of the Central Committee, elected at Evanston, is Dr Franklin Clark Fry, a Lutheran, of the United States; the General Secretary is still the Dutch Calvinist clergyman, Wisser t' Hooft, a theologian of Barthian leanings and the moving spirit of the whole Ecumenical Council.

The Central Committee holds important meetings periodically. The first after Amsterdam took place at Chichester under the presidency of Dr Bell with a hundred people present for six days, July 9th–15th, 1949.[1]

The next meeting was held at Toronto in July 1950. Dr Wisser t' Hooft read an important report which assessed the achievements of the Council of Churches. The advantages of the Movement were better relations among the Churches, which were even able to influence theological thought[2]; reciprocal help; united intervention in international public life; collaboration in missionary work.

Opposition arises, internally, because the communities fear that they may be led further than they want to go, and also because of a revival of sectarianism; externally, opposition arises from over-hasty judgements which accuse the movement of communist tendencies or dogmatic intransigence. The report defined what was required for membership of the Ecumenical Council: "to seek earnestly and steadfastly ways and means to declare the essential unity of the Church of Christ".[3]

During the same meeting, a report was presented called *The Church of Churches, and the World Council of Churches,* in which the nature of the Council was defined. It is not a super-Church and it does not imply any particular conception of Church, or of unity. The following important principle was accepted: a Church may be a member of the Council even if it

---

[1] *Ecumenical Review,* II (1949–50), pp. 35 following. Hereafter quoted as *ER.*
[2] *ER,* III (1950–1), pp. 53 following.
[3] *Ibid.,* p. 57.

proclaims itself to be the only true Church, and therefore does not consider the other member-Churches as Churches in the full sense of the word.[4] In fact, the Greek Orthodox delegates at the Assembly at Evanston declared that their Church was the only legitimate one.

Other important meetings of the Central Committee aimed at settling special questions, such as the world refugee problem (at Bayreuth, in May 1951), or to prepare for the second Assembly of Evanston.

In 1952, an important event took place, the Conference held at Lund, in Sweden, which was organized by the Faith and Order Commission; for this Conference careful preparation was made by means of publications written by the best specialists. The direction taken by this Conference was rather in favour of the tendency defined by the Amsterdam Assembly as "catholic", by which word they mean faith in the apostolic succession of the bishops, and the power of the sacraments. The authors were favourable to the idea of the sacraments, and to a special priesthood, to the real presence of Christ in the Eucharist, to the admission of a eucharistic sacrifice, to the baptism of children, and to a definite liturgy. As to the nature of the Church, they hoped that a better understanding of dogma would lessen the different conceptions of it.

The Conference lasted from August 18th to 29th, and there were more than 320 delegates and observers from forty countries. The vicar apostolic of Sweden (now bishop of Stockholm) had designated four observers from the same place. The German Catholics, at a meeting in Berlin, sent fraternal good wishes to the Conference.

Apparently the members of the Conference did not follow the suggestions published by preparatory commissions. It is true that they unanimously approved the report, which they followed about various questions, particularly on the conception of the Church, the so-called "catholic" direction; but the conclusions of the Conference, which occupied the first chapter of the

[4] *Ibid.*, p. 51.

report, are much vaguer. At the second Conference, perhaps the most important one, the delegates affirm that they have understood that the way to unity will be found, not by comparing their ideas and traditions, but by uniting themselves more closely with Christ. United to Christ, they will be united amongst themselves.

Some thought that in the Faith and Order Commission the more "Protestant" tendencies had won. The future will decide that. Meanwhile, it was resolved that henceforward the Commission was to be composed of eighty members, elected by the World Council, which meets every three years. But a special Committee of twenty-two members, elected from within it, was to meet each year.[5] One of the present problems of the W.C.C. is the position to give to the Faith and Order Commission. In 1939 it was still one of the two groups which together constituted the W.C.C. After the agreements of Evanston (1954), it is only one of five departments of a division of the W.C.C. (and there are four divisions). It desired to have the name and importance of a division. Its function is of fundamental importance in the W.C.C. because it should lead the Churches of the W.C.C. to the real visible unity of the Church of Christ.[6]

THE SECOND ASSEMBLY AT EVANSTON

At Evanston the number of Churches represented was 163, a slightly larger number than at Amsterdam in 1948. The 600 delegates came from forty-eight countries and with accredited visitors, observers and journalists, the assembly consisted of about 1,300 people. All the most powerful weapons of publicity were used; a visit from Eisenhower, a spectacular festival, telegraph, radio and television. Eight tons of paper were used. It became necessary to divide the members into many groups to study the different subjects, and so it was very difficult to

[5] On the Lund Conference, see *Unitas* (Italian ed., Nuova Serie), I (1952), pp. 3–7, 29–33, 152–5; II (1953), pp. 1–4.

[6] See *The Ecumenical Review*, April 1959, and *The Future of Faith and Order*, by Keith R. Bridston, pp. 249–58.

follow the general proceedings of the Assembly. The useful work was chiefly done during the preparations. The Assembly was more concerned with demonstrating the unity of the members, and with the fact of the existence of the Ecumenical Council.

Cardinal Stritch of Chicago, in whose diocese Evanston lies, published a pastoral letter in which he explained why the Catholic Church was not taking part in the Assembly, saying: "She must not take part in any organization or assembly at which representatives of various denominations meet to discuss, on equal terms, the nature of the Church of Christ, the nature of the unity of the Church, or even the possibility of bringing Christians back to unity, and making plans for 'united Christian action'.

"Catholics," Cardinal Stritch continued, "were unable to take part in any activity, or assist at any conference or discussion, based on the erroneous supposition that the Catholic Church was still seeking the fullness of Christian truths. Such a search would be to admit that the Catholic Church was only one of the various forms which represent, or do not represent, the true Church of Christ, and that she, in her present form, does not possess that unity of faith, hierarchy and community, desired by our Lord; and that she still does not understand the true idea and the true nature of this unity and of those other qualities desired by God, which distinguish her not only as *a Church* but as *a holy Catholic and apostolic Church,* founded by our Lord and Saviour Jesus Christ. Such a supposition cannot possibly be admitted by the Church, because she is today what she has always been, the one and only spouse of Christ, the one and only Body of Christ, and the one and only Church of Christ. It cannot be admitted that the unity desired by our Lord for this Church has never existed, and does not exist now."

The main theme before the Assembly was: "Christ, the hope of the world." The choice of this theme was very significant. It did not require the Assembly to study the means to promote the unity of Christians, which is the whole purpose of the Ecumenical Council, but it used the Council to proclaim together a Christian truth. The idea of collaboration replaced, or at least took precedence over, that of unity.

Two opposite tendencies became obvious during the discussion of the main theme. Is Christ the hope of the world for the purpose of obtaining temporal goods, such as peace, prosperity and liberty, or for the eternal happiness of the next world, which will be given to all at the last judgement of the *parousia*? Dr. Schink, of Heidelberg, insisted on the eschatological point of view. "If in our reflections on this subject, we were to place the accent on the salvation of this doomed world, we would have completely misunderstood the true meaning of the theme of the Assembly", he said. But an American delegate, Dr Calhoun, of Yale, insisted on the presence of hope in Christ in this world, although he did not forget to mention the obvious limitations of such an attitude. There was evident tension between these two tendencies in the fifteen groups into which the delegates were divided to study the theme. It was not possible to change the text presented to the Assembly, but in recommending it to the Churches, a statement was added in which many criticisms are expressed, some of which are of real importance. For example, disagreement is admitted about the relationship of Christian hope, here and now, and the fulfilment of it at the end of time.

The question of unity, however, was touched upon by the Assembly in various ways. To start with, the very fact of the present divisions gave rise to consideration of it. One of the six secondary themes, that of the Faith and Order Commission, was called "Our unity in Christ and our division as Churches". The report presented to the Commission, and later accepted by the full meeting, develops these three ideas: the Churches possess unity in as much as they relate to Christ, who is one; the guilty state of their divisions does not prevent that unity in Christ, just as in the Lutheran doctrine the state of being a sinner does not prevent justification, that is the application of the justice of Christ; but it is a duty of the Churches to display their unity and make it more evident.

The chief aids suggested for growth in unity were: meditation in common on the Bible, the struggle against non-theological reasons for the divisions, and prayer.

But that report did not receive the assent of the Orthodox delegation, which declared that such a way of considering the problem of reunion was unacceptable. Christian faith, said the Greek-Orthodox delegate, must be accepted as a whole; the Bible is not the only organ of revelation, for apostolic tradition is another; the Holy Spirit assists and guides the Church; the bishops are necessary and should descend from the apostles by succession. Unity should be re-established now, without waiting for the end of the world. The Church is never sinful, but unspotted, despite the sins of her members. She is infallible.

Five other groups studied the special reports on evangelization, on social problems, on international affairs, and on the laity.

Before adjourning, the Assembly unanimously approved a message which summed up the results of their work. Here are the most important points:

2. This time of crisis which we are undergoing is full of hopes and fears. It is a good thing to hope for liberty, justice and peace, because God desires us to have those good things. But he has created us for a higher end. He has made us for himself, to know him and love him, to adore him and to serve him. God alone can satisfy the heart of man. He who forgets this is his own worst enemy; he searches for justice but creates injustice; he aspires towards peace, but moves towards war. His command of nature becomes a threat of ruin. Whether he realizes it or not, he is exposed to the justice of God, in the shadow of death.

3. Jesus Christ lived like us in our own conditions. True God and true man, he came to seek us out and save us. Even if we were his enemies, he died for us. We have crucified him, but God raised him up from the dead. He overcame the power of sin and of death, and a new life started. By the power of his resurrection and ascension, he has established a new community in the world, united in his spirit, participating in his divine life, with the task of spreading the knowledge of him throughout the world. He will return as our judge and king, to accomplish all

things. Then we shall see him as he is, and we shall know him, as we are known by him. . . .

6. We want to turn now to each single community. Six years ago our Churches took on the task of forming this Ecumenical Council, and declared that they wanted to remain united. We thank God for his blessing on our work and on our communion during these six years. We start now on the second lap of our journey. It is not enough to remain together; we must go forward. The more we become aware of our unity in Christ, so much the less can we tolerate our divisions. Therefore we put this question: Has your Church seriously considered its relationship with the other Churches in the light of the Lord's Prayer, so that we may be sanctified in truth and may all be one? Is your community in communion with the other communities which surround it, making every effort so that each one may hear the voice of the only Shepherd who calls all men to form one single fold?

The future will decide whether the Assembly of Evanston has helped towards the reunion of Christians. In any case, it has at least helped to keep alive the idea of unity. Once ideas are disseminated in many minds, they do not remain fruitless.

AFTER EVANSTON

Various events of interest to the ecumenical movement have occurred between the Assembly of Evanston and the present day.

In 1955 partial intercommunion was approved by the two Convocations of Canterbury and York, between the Church of England and the union formed in South India of four denominations: Anglicans, Presbyterians, Methodists and Congregationalists. The basis of the union was the acceptance by them all of the episcopate; from now on all the ministers would be ordained by one bishop. However, belief in any precise doctrine of episcopacy was not required; meanwhile all ministers functioning at the time were immediately recognized by the whole Church.

The method by which this union was achieved became accepted as a guide for similar unions. In a rather similar way, various other unions were planned, one for Ceylon (the Lanka scheme of Church Union in Ceylon), another for North India and Pakistan (Church Union in North India and Pakistan); and negotiations are in progress to unite the Church of England and the Nonconformists, chiefly the Presbyterian Church of Scotland.

These unions are judged very differently. The pilot-union, as that of South India was called, was praised by some, either because it abolishes divisions, or because the non-Anglican denominations have accepted a more positive form, that is the episcopate. Others, however, think that Anglican doctrine suffers in various ways: ministers are accepted *ad interim* who have not been ordained by a bishop, the episcopate is not considered to be sacramental by many, and the Church thus united appears to be a new confession, or at least a new denomination which does not do away with the others. Almost all recognize that the constitution of South India has the disadvantages inherent in compromises, disadvantages which are particularly serious in the religious field.[7]

After Evanston, the World Council of Churches considered at its meetings an important decision: whether to unite with the International Missionary Council, which was founded to help the Protestant missions. The decision to integrate the two bodies was taken at the New Delhi Assembly in 1961 (see Appendix). Both the Orthodox members of the Council and the Catholics, who are not members but are interested in ecumenism, consider that such a step is not ecumenical, because it makes the Council, which was established to work for Christian unity, the supporter of one side and propagator of division.

---

[7] In favour of the CSI is Eric L. Mascall, *The Convocation and South India* (London, Mowbray, 1955), and Donald Rea, *The Church of South India and the Church* (Oxford, 1956). With reservations but sympathy, L. Bouyer, "L'Union des Églises du Sud de l'Inde", *Istina* II (1955), pp. 215–37, and M. Villain, *Introduction à l'oecuménisme* (Paris-Tournai, Casterman, 1958), pp. 66–71. Against are the Anglo-Catholic Annunciation Group, and, among others, various authors in *Unitas*, 1958, pp. 208–13.

It is possible that the direction taken by the W.C.C. was not without influence on the resolution made at the full synod of the Orthodox Church of Greece in November 1958, which reads thus: "Our Church has been obliged to have some reservations as to the participation in the meetings of the Protestant Ecumenical Movement. She has decided that this participation cannot be of members of the clergy, but only of lay theologians. And further, their participation at these meetings can only be allowed if precise instructions are followed and on the condition that the Protestant world discontinues propaganda which is detrimental to the faithful of our Orthodox Church."

CHAPTER IV

REASONS FOR HOPE

We know now, at least in broad outline, the present state of those Christian communities which are separated from the Roman Church in their attitude to unity. It is time now to indicate the reasons for hoping for a better situation in the not too distant future. These reasons, unfortunately, do not show us any sudden change, but considered as a whole they allow us, or rather advise us, oblige us and compel us to work for the reconciliation of Christians, according to the will of the common Master. Many of these reasons are deduced from very recent events and could not have been formulated half a century ago.

The great division is that which separates Roman Catholics from the other Christians. The Protestant professor, Oscar Cullman, declares it thus: "I am increasingly of mind that the results achieved at Geneva should not allow us to lose sight for one moment of the essential ecumenical problem, which is that of the relationship between Roman Christianity and non-Roman Christianity."[1] Now there are signs that the non-Catholics are approaching closer to the doctrines and practices of the Roman Catholic Church.

THE PROTESTANT POSITION

The desire for unity

The first sign is in the non-Catholic movements seeking unity. We have not concealed their wavering, their difficulties and even their near failures; but we must recognize that they

[1] Oscar Cullmann, *Catholiques et Protestants, Un projet de solidarité chrétienne* (Delachaux et Niestlé, Neufchâtel-Paris, 1958), pp. 9–10.

have changed the general atmosphere, not only of relationships among non-Catholics, but also with the Roman Church.

The very existence of the Ecumenical Council, and the desire for unity which inspires all the members in varying degrees, are today the result of efforts towards greater unity of non-Catholics. An organization to demonstrate and to promote the best possible understanding among such numerous and different denominations is in fact a great innovation. Undoubtedly one danger could have arisen; that of achieving unity by forming a single front against Rome. But that would have been contrary to the "ecumenical" ideal. In any case, the sincere intention of the present leaders of the Council is to seek a way of establishing good relations with the Roman Catholic Church.

There is too, in the heart of the Council, keeping a certain independence, the Faith and Order group, with an organization in charge of dogmatic studies concerning problems of unity. Why should we not have faith in the power of truth? Why should we not hope that objective thought, dispelling prejudice and misunderstandings, should bring those souls of good will closer to the Church of Rome?

The problem is, in fact, correctly stated. Both Boegner and Wisser t' Hooft amongst the Protestants, like Florovsky amongst the Orthodox, define the unity of the Church as unity in the same faith. Boegner, who is one of the most authoritative spokesmen of French Protestantism, has written on "the problem of Christian unity", meaning the unity of faith and visible unity. It is this unity which he has found in the sacred Scriptures. The witnesses, he says

> are there, in sacred Scripture, entrusted with a revelation which the Holy Spirit affirms as the truth of God. Whether we like it or not, they speak of only one Church of Christ, the visible unity of which is part of the testimony which it must render to the Lord. Just as there is only one Lord, only one faith, only one baptism, only one God and Father of all, and only one Spirit and only one hope, so there is one body,[2] only one Church.[3]

[2] Cf. Ephes. 4. 4.
[3] *Le Problème de l'Unité Chrétienne* (Paris, 1947), p. 129.

It is true that the very people who think that the Church of Christ ought to be one, and understand that that unity requires the same faith, despair of seeing the Lord's plan realized in this world, and postpone the existence of one Church to the end of the world; but such a position is untenable. Jesus Christ was clearly referring to the Church on earth when he desired that his disciples should be one, as the Father and Son are one. Either Christ is powerless, which no Christian can think, or there really does exist on the earth the Church for which Christ prayed.

The hope of Catholics can, therefore, be expressed thus: the leaders of Protestantism today recognize that Christ wanted unity of faith in his Church; but unity of faith is only to be found in the Catholic Church; therefore, the day will come when Protestants must confess that the Catholic Church is the one founded by Christ.

There is an even more powerful reason for hoping for progress towards unity in modern Protestantism, which is the faith in Jesus Christ recognized as God made man. We are well aware that many so-called liberal Protestants, who are really rationalists, continue to reject this fundamental truth of Christianity, but the Ecumenical Council has made the divinity of Christ the doctrinal basis which all its members must accept: "The Ecumenical Council is composed of those Churches which recognize Jesus Christ as God and Saviour."

The Evanston Assembly has unanimously proclaimed exactly this profession of faith in its message:

> Jesus Christ lived with us. He came to us, true God and true Man, to seek us out and save us. Although we were enemies of God, he died for us. We have crucified him, but God has raised him up from the dead. He is risen. He has conquered the power of sin and death. A new life has started. By the power of his resurrection and his ascension, he has sent into the whole world a new community united by his Spirit, who participate in his divine life, and who are entrusted in making it known in the world. He will return as judge and king to lead all things to fulfilment. Then, we shall see him as he is, and we shall know him as we are known.

This profession of faith is of the utmost importance. It cannot be objected that Luther believed in the divinity of Christ, and that did not prevent the disunity which we today would like to abolish, because Luther used all his resources to propagate his own new ideas and was not concerned with emphasizing what he kept in common with Catholics. Today, on the contrary, the members of the Ecumenical Council, finding themselves in a state of division which they have not created and the disadvantages of which they deplore, are willing to start from what they hold in common and to increase that further so as to eliminate, if possible, every important difference. To people of such a disposition the worship of Jesus Christ cannot fail to make them hate divisions and, at the same time, to help them to advance towards unity. Indeed, it is very painful to see a man, who considers that he loves and adores Jesus, interpret the chief words of the Saviour in a completely different way. At least that is what a Catholic feels when he meets someone who adores Christ with all his soul, and yet declares that he belongs to another Church.

Two brothers are more upset by their disagreements when they consider their common love for their mother. The love of Jesus makes the unhappy separation of Christians felt; so that it makes unity desirable and urges man to achieve it. In fact, it is very significant that in Jesus' prayer to the Father for the unity of his disciples, he clearly indicated that belief in his divinity was the natural bond of that unity.[4] "I have given them the message which thou gavest to me, and they receiving it, recognized it for truth that I came from thee, and found faith to believe that it was thou who didst send me."[5] And again: "And I have given them the privilege which thou gavest to me, that they should all be one, as we are one."[6] This glory, which they will see in heaven,[7] is that which the Son received before

[4] See R. Matzerath, S.A., *The Prayer of Christ for Unity* (Rome, 1950).
[5] John 17. 8.
[6] John 17. 22.
[7] John 17. 24.

the creation of the world. It is the divine nature which he who is called Father ("I have revealed thy name to them"[8]) gives him eternally. Belief in the divinity of Christ, especially where it expands in love and where nothing opposes its natural influence, inclines one towards belief in everything which is in harmony with it; and so from this fundamental dogma flow all the truths which the Incarnate Word has revealed and all that he has instituted. For in the Good Tidings everything is arranged so much better and more harmoniously than in the ways invented by man. From the divinity of Christ, which already implies all the mysteries of the Holy Trinity, of the Incarnation and Redemption, one is led on to the Church and the sacraments as to an expected conclusion and providential continuation of the work of salvation. From the adoration of the Son, the way is open to the cult of his heavenly Mother. The action of the Saviour himself, sincerely and if necessary bravely confessed, will work towards bringing his adorers to the fullness of the faith, and from that also towards the union of all in one integral *Credo*. If the Ecumenical Council succeeds in maintaining in the forefront of its meetings the luminous image of God made man, it will have done good work towards that unity, the search for which is the reason for its existence.

Changes of ideas

An important reason for hoping for the return of many sects of the Reformation to the ancient faith lies in the great changes which have come about since the first years of the sixteenth century. More than once, Protestants have said to us: "The reasons which separate us today are no longer those which brought about the break." Who indeed would refer to those many accusations which weighed so heavily in the controversies of that time? After the admirable series of popes whom God has given to his Church, such as Pius VI and Pius VII who were willing to suffer for Christ in prison, and those like Pius

[8] John 17. 26.

IX and Pius X who bravely resisted modern impiety, and those who from Leo XIII to the reigning pontiff have shed a most beneficial light on modern problems by their teaching, and who have always led an exemplary life, sometimes reaching real sanctity, who would take up again Luther's attacks on the papacy? Far from following the leaders of the Reformation in their action against the religious life, many Anglicans have united under the Rule of St Benedict or of St Francis of Assisi, and the Calvinists of Taizé in France follow them.

Turning to doctrine, we find that the principle of the sufficiency of Scripture is no longer the only one admitted. A certain amount of tradition is recognized as valid by the Anglicans, as also by the school called *Geschichtliche Formschule*. On the questions of liberty and predestination, there are very few who uphold without exception the theses of Luther and Calvin. Today we often find the Protestant mentality closer to Pelagius than to the Augustinian monk of Wittenberg. Newman was still far from the Catholic Church when he hung a picture of the Blessed Virgin upon the walls of his brother's bedroom. It is really surprising for us to see books published with Protestant names, so close to our own attitudes, dealing with our Lady, confession, tradition, the power given to St Peter, perpetual celibacy, etc. Those who want to live a really "reformed" Christian life, that is full of earnestness, dignity and detachment from the world, know that they will find it in the heart of Catholicism. Also the violence and hatred which were let loose in the religious wars have now died down. The tone of the discussions and controversies is, in the majority of cases, irenic. In short, it is possible to think that today the disunity is nothing but a heavy legacy of history. Can one not hope, then, that many will refuse to bear this yoke of the past any longer, which was formed by the decisions of a few men of another age, and, in any case, for reasons which have now lost their force?

In fact, important groups are moving towards the Roman Church. The Oxford Movement, which resulted in the conversion of Newman and of so many of his friends, has not yet finished producing results. From it developed Anglo-Catholicism which shows a marked approach to Roman Catholicism, especially in certain elements. Within it are published books, such as those of Spencer Jones, which are nothing but an ardent and justified appeal to reject the word of a bad king and to reunite with the See of Peter, as desired by Christ himself. There are Anglo-Catholic societies who are urging the return to Rome and who work by means of publishing well-written magazines such as *Reunion* and *Pilot*. These are groups who recognize no valid reason for staying outside the Catholic Church other than that of waiting for the others, so that they may now return together, just as they left together.

We have seen how the Lambeth Conference favoured the formation in South India of a Church in which the Anglican community was united to non-episcopal Churches, and how the archbishop of Canterbury seeks unity with the Nonconformists. This liberalism is painfully disquieting to the Anglo-Catholics and drives them towards Rome.

However, in Anglo-Catholicism, there is a tendency which is opposed to reunion. The whole movement seems to have reached a crossroad. If it elects to go to Rome, it will save the faith of its members and reach that goal which Providence seems to have prepared for over a century. If, on the other hand, it tends towards liberalism, it will be lost and will hasten the dechristianization of the Church of England, that disaster so much feared by Newman. Catholics hope that so many prayers offered up for England must obtain that at least the majority of Anglo-Catholics will follow where Newman led.

One must remember that the Anglo-Catholic frame of mind is not found only in Great Britain but also, under other names, in other countries, such as North America, South Africa and Sweden. From thence came the impetus for the Ecumenical Council, and the profession of faith in the divinity of Christ. It will remain true to itself, therefore, if it opposes the liberal and modernistic tendencies which threaten to overthrow the Church of England.

In Sweden, one of the Lutheran strongholds, a ritualist movement has arisen which, in spite of the condemnations of Luther,
resumes the celebration of the Mass understood as a sacrifice.
Dutch Calvinism is torn by major controversies. In 1950, a
group of clergymen published a declaration in which they uphold, among other things, the necessity of Tradition and of an
apostolic ordination for the administration of the sacraments.
A Swiss clergyman, Roger Schutz, conceived the idea of intro-
ducing the monastic life into Calvinism. Together with his
friend, Max Thurian, he has established in France, at Taizé,
near the old Benedictine abbey of Cluny, a community in
which already over thirty religious have made vows of poverty,
chastity and obedience; they celebrate the liturgical offices in
common and work for Christian unity.

Germany is in a state of intense agitation. The Nazi persecution made Catholics and Protestants unite in resistance; during
the war both creeds were persecuted; and after the war a
political party grew up, the Christian Democrat Party, composed of Catholics and Protestants. This party has saved the
denominational State School. These contacts also provoked
interdenominational discussions among theologians. A richer
liturgical life, centred on the altar, has penetrated among the
Lutherans. A Lutheran theologian, Asmussen, has written a
book on the Blessed Virgin which is very close to the Catholic
attitude. He belongs to a group, *Die Sammlung,* which is working against disunity. At Darmstadt a convent has been founded
with over fifty nuns who have taken the name of "Sisters of
Mary". Finally, the conversion of the clergyman, Goethe, a
descendant of the poet, was the logical outcome of a Christian
life dedicated to the search for the fullness of faith. Almost the
whole group to which he belonged has come into the Catholic
Church. On this occasion, Pius XII showed his sympathetic
interest and kindness by allowing this married convert to be
ordained a priest.

All these events show that the prayers and efforts towards
unity are not without effect. They permit us to hope that some
day the great divisions of the past will be healed.

The Times *and the Roman Church*

On October 31st, 1949, *The Times* of London published an article by a special correspondent on the relationship of Rome with the rest of the Christian world. The author expressed sorrow at the divisions which weaken the work of believers, recognized the eminent position and world-wide influence of the Roman Church, and called for a conference to be convoked, composed of Catholic and Protestant theologians, to reach agreement on essential matters.

The article created a stir. In England, and elsewhere, the newspapers wrote at length about it. Many letters were addressed to the editor of *The Times*. These letters constituted a real and passionate public controversy between Catholics and Anglicans. On November 29th, the newspaper closed the discussion, with an editorial article of the same inspiration as that of the original article. Afterwards, articles and letters were published in an interesting booklet under the title of *Catholicism Today*.

This was an important dialogue between Catholics and Protestants. The first article showed a friendly spirit and a real desire for an understanding with the Catholic hierarchy, the better to combat today's enemy, atheistic materialism. But it did not only deal with a practical agreement for common action on a specialized ground, such as existed in various countries during the war, and especially in England, with for example, the interdenominational society, the Sword of the Spirit; rather it dealt with the defining of the essential doctrines on which agreement might be reached, leaving the remainder to the free choice of the Churches. Now, if the points considered unessential consisted only of such things as the forms of the liturgy, and certain private attitudes of some Catholics, an agreement could surely be reached; but it is more likely that they were thinking of doctrines which the Roman Church has already defined as being revealed by God, and in that case the duty of Catholics is not only to profess them with the firmest faith, but also not to be in communion with those who deny them.

As one of the correspondents, Mgr G. A. Beck, then coad-jutor bishop of Brentwood, now bishop of Salford, said, quoting the encyclical *Mortalium animos*: "There is no difference be-tween the Catholic's acceptance of the doctrine of the Immacu-late Conception and his belief in the divinity of Christ. To him both propositions are true because they have been revealed by God."[9]

The discussion which took place in the letters following the article by the "special correspondent" showed the existence of pessimists and optimists. The pessimists consisted of both Pro-testants who accused Rome of unbearable totalitarianism, and of Catholics who saw no meeting-point for a real and efficaci-ous understanding. Nevertheless, there were more encouraging voices on both sides, those who emphasized the divine omni-potence and the prayer of Jesus for unity among those who be-lieve in him, or those who agreed that conversations between competent people in a friendly atmosphere tended more to-wards full mutual understanding than bitter controversy.

The final article in *The Times* definitely adopts the latter point of view. In fact, the author concluded that the most promising step would be a meeting of theologians of different views, whose deliberations would be held in private but would later be published. He added that, meanwhile, those questions of morality which are endangered today and on which there is agreement, should be collected so that they may be proclaimed as of common assent.

This event shows how the Protestants feel their weakness when faced with the anti-Christian powers, and how they recognize ever more fully the strength which the Catholic Church owes to her constitution. It may be the dawn of better times.

The dialogue continues

The charges which the Protestants usually bring against the Catholic Church are varied, according to the different positions

[9] *Catholicism Today*, p. 31.

of the denominations. At Evanston, Dr Reinhold Niebuhr insisted on the Lutheran doctrine of grace, and accused the Roman Church of intervening between God and men, of recognizing meritorious works, and of wanting to rule men by the priesthood. Catholics answer that the Church was founded by Jesus Christ with the power of the keys of the kingdom, and that it is not an obstacle but a means of salvation for mankind.

The Anglicans usually request that a distinction be made between essential and non-essential dogmas, so that by leaving adherence or not to the non-essential dogmas free, unity could be achieved. But this attitude, Catholics point out, destroys the ideas of faith and authority. The Church is bound to demand the acceptance of all that God has revealed. Now God has not only revealed the fundamental dogmas, such as the Holy Trinity and the Incarnation, but also all that the Church believes to be of divine faith, the infallibility of the Church and of the Roman Pontiff, the Immaculate Conception of the Blessed Virgin and her Assumption, etc. Whoever refuses to believe any one of the truths revealed by God no longer obeys the reason for his faith which is the authority of a God who has made a definite revelation.

The definition of the Assumption of Mary was the occasion for many Protestants to condemn the privileged position which the Roman Catholic Church has given to the Mother of God. They repeat that, according to Scripture, there is only one Mediator, Jesus Christ. Catholics reply that the function of Mediatrix which they attribute to our Lady is one of the effects obtained by the mediation of Christ, and that her function remains always subordinate to and dependent on the mediation of Christ.

THE EAST

These reasons for hoping that the efforts towards unity will reach important results concern Protestantism. If now we turn towards the East, we certainly find in these dissident Churches formidable obstacles to unity, but also more helpful things than in Protestantism.

In fact, first of all, there exists a long past of nine or even eleven centuries (since the schism did not become definite until Michael Cerularius), and a past which we have in common, recognized and accepted by both sides, and of which we are both justifiably proud. Since that time, the Orthodox Churches have not been able to define anything, because they admitted that they were unable to convoke an Ecumenical Council and, moreover, they do not admit any supreme authority capable of defining the truths of the faith. The Roman Church, on the other hand, has definitely proclaimed a certain number of truths, but these truths are either already well known since the eleventh century, or else they arise from a more distinct understanding of what was then only implicit. Further, one can always find Orthodox theologians who have upheld the opinions which the Church later defined as dogmas. One must, therefore, allow that Jugie is right when he asserts that there are fewer obstacles to unity with the East.

Apart from such instrinsically greater helps, recent events have shown the weakness of those separated Churches before the temporal powers, to which they are subject because of their isolation and their traditions. So much so that the Czar of all the Russias called himself the defender of Orthodoxy, believing and praying like his people. The dependence of the Russian Church on him was certainly not without difficulties, but at least it was in accordance with the integrity of the doctrine and the essential dignity of the priesthood. But when power passed into the hands of an atheistic government, whose programme includes as a fundamental point the suppression of every religion, how can there possibly be any understanding with it, and how can the Churches maintain their dignity by becoming its instrument? To praise without reservation the Soviet power, to help it in its campaign against the Catholic Church, to collaborate with it in the acts of violence directed against the Uniates, to refrain from protesting against the antireligious proclamations and decrees, all this shows the degeneration of pastors of souls who refuse to accept the authority of the successor of Peter, and submit to the orders and directions of atheists with every appearance of satisfaction. Such a phenomenon emphasizes the Church's need for an independent spiritual head who can defend the rights of the Church, wherever they are attacked. It is obvious that only the pope today has a sufficiently widespread and powerful authority for this. At the time of the Conversations at Malines, Canon Hemmer concluded his work on the relationship of the pope and the bishops, considered from an historical point of view, with these important words: "No Church should want to deprive itself of the supreme source which in certain cases can only be found in the supreme power of the Head of the universal Church."[10] Indeed, the contrast between the passivity of the Synod of Moscow and the brave resistance of the Catholic bishops, of a Stepinac, a Mindszenty, a Beran, and of so many other bishops, cannot leave the East unmoved, and will undoubtedly help to determine, at an early date, a genuine movement for the return to Catholic unity.

There are already signs of the desire which many of our separated brethren of the East feel for a union of which the bishop of Rome would be the bond. It is true that they conceive of this bond in a way which is still too vague and too liberal; but the fact that they turn towards the pope is a sign of the times.[11] The Russian emigrants, especially, have shown on various occasions a real desire for unity. May all these heirs of a glorious antiquity understand that they would simply be following their ancestors by recognizing in the successor of Peter, the office of supreme shepherd, with the rights and power which such a title means.

Finally, the attitude of the separated Eastern Churches towards the World Council of Churches is not without interest. Either they refuse all collaboration, and by that show their attachment to dogma and preserve themselves more securely from Protestant infiltrations, which are so opposed to their

[10] Jacques de Bivort de la Saudée, *Documents sur le problème de l'union anglo-romaine (1921–1927)* (Paris, 1949), p. 211.

[11] See, for example in *Unitas*, I (1946), p. 91, an interesting article by the Rumanian metropolitan Visarion. See also in *Unitas*, IV (1949), pp. 228 *et seq.*

spirit (even when political influences seem fairly obvious in their hostile declarations to the Council, the religious reason is still present and its importance is felt); or else a few isolated groups agree to go to the ecumenical conferences, but they show a courageous intransigence on questions of doctrine, and they sometimes recall plainly that true ecumenical unity cannot be achieved without the Roman Catholic Church. Professor Florovsky of the Russian Church, for example, declared it at Amsterdam[12] and at Evanston. How could they admit union with the Protestants, so different from themselves, and not seek unity with Rome, which is so close?

The chief enemy of true unity is indifference; all those who resist it, or even fight it, are working for unity.

THE EFFORTS OF THE ROMAN CHURCH

However real and active the efforts towards unity may be outside the Church, yet it is still in the Roman Church that we find the deepest and strongest desire to take back to herself those who have left her. Would she be truly a mother if she forgot her children? Even in official documents, the style of which is usually rather austere, one can feel the beating of a heart full of regrets, pain and hopes when considering disunity. Not forgetting the numerous popes who have especially worked for the reconciliation of the dissident Christians and whom Leo XIII once named Innocent III, Eugene IV, Julius III, the three Gregorys, X, XIII, XV, Urban VIII and others[13]—we can listen to what the modern popes have to say.[14] Already in 1948, Pius IX addressed a passionate appeal to the Eastern Churches separated from the Roman communion, assuring them that nothing would be required of them beyond what was required by the unity of faith.[15] At the Vatican Council, the Protestants

[12] See *Unitas*, IV (1949), p. 88.

[13] Allocution of March 3rd, 1896.

[14] Cf. A. Brunello, "La S. Sede e l'Unione delle Chiese", in *Unitas*, II (1947), pp. 339–54; III (1948), pp. 124–43.

[15] Letter "In Suprema Petri Apostoli Sede" in *Acta Apostolicae Sedis*, I, pp. 154–61.

as well as the Easterns were invited to return to unity. Thus was at least recalled the duty of the supreme shepherd to seek out the erring, and the duty of these to return to the fold.

Leo XIII worked very hard for the return of the separated East. He considered in 1897 that one of the two great aims of his long pontificate had been and still was "to promote the reunion of those who have fallen away from the Catholic Church either by heresy or by schism, since it is most undoubtedly the will of Christ that all should be united in one flock under one Shepherd".[16]

During the first years of his pontificate, the political situation gave him much hope in that direction. He multiplied his appeals and enterprises. He used to say: "It is by no means shameful that the Father should call home his sons who have strayed away, and who have waited for so long. We must go out to meet them and stretch out our arms to clasp those who are returning to our hearts".[17] His pressing appeals cannot be read without emotion in the encyclical *Praeclara gratulationis* to the Easterns[18]: "Weigh carefully in your minds and before God the nature of our request. It is not for any human motive, but impelled by divine charity and a desire for the salvation of all, that we advise the reconciliation and union with the Church of Rome"; and he recalled the words of Bessarion: "What are we going to say to the Lord when he asks us to render an account of this separation from our brothers, he who came down from Heaven to unite us in one fold, who was made flesh and was crucified?" Then he said to the Protestants: "Our heart appeals to you even more than our words, to you, our brethren, who for three centuries and more differ from us on Christian faith; and to you all likewise who in later times for any reason whatsoever have turned away from us. Let us all meet in the unity of faith and of the knowledge of the Son of God."

Then followed the encyclical *Orientalium dignitas* which

[16] Encyclical, *Divinum illud munus*.
[17] Letter to the Armenians, *Paterna Caritas*, June 25th, 1888, in *AAS*, XXI, pp. 374–78.
[18] June 29th, 1894, in *AAS*, XXVI, pp. 705–17.

ordered the preservation of the Oriental rites,[19] and the encyclical *Christi nomen*,[20] which recommended the formation of a Catholic clergy to lead the Eastern Churches to the unity of the faith. Leo XIII encouraged them in this effort saying: "It is there, alive in the Gospel, the sweet and reassuring promise of the Saviour: There shall be one fold and one Shepherd."[21] And he appointed a Commission *ad Reconciliationem Dissidentium cum Ecclesia fovendam*.[22]

But Leo XIII also looked towards the West. On hearing of the efforts of Lord Halifax and other Anglo-Catholics, he wrote a moving letter *ad Anglos*[23] to encourage the good will of those pioneers of unity, and to exhort the Catholics to pray with confidence for the reconciliation of their compatriots. For his part, he explained the doctrine of the unity of the Church in an important encyclical, *Satis cognitum*. Shortly afterwards, he had to confirm solemnly the traditional doctrine of the Church concerning the invalidity of Anglican orders.[24] But he continued until the end of his long pontificate to promote the return of all Christians to the unity of the faith. The Commission which he established for that purpose did not survive him, but the novena of prayers still exists, that novena which he ordered to be celebrated in all churches before the feast of Pentecost, "to promote the reunion of those who have fallen away from the Catholic Church either by heresy or by schism, since it is most undoubtedly the will of Christ that all should be united in one flock under one Shepherd".[25] It was certainly one of the most noble achievements of that great pope to have denounced solemnly to the world the evil of disunity, and to have worked with such perseverance to heal it.

In 1909, Pius X approved the octave of prayers for unity, the

[19] *AAS*, XXVII, pp. 257–64.
[20] *Ibid.*, pp. 385–93.
[21] Allocution of March 2nd, 1895.
[22] March 19th, 1895.
[23] April 14th, 1895.
[24] Apostolic Letter: *Apostolicae curae*, September 15th, 1896.
[25] Encyclicals: *Provida Matris*, May 5th, 1895; *Divinum illud*, May 9th, 1897.

practice of which was spread by the Protestant convert, Paul Watson. Benedict XV encouraged the same octave with indulgences. This pope, whose pontificate was all too brief, created two great Institutions, which are by their nature designed to work for the reunion of the East; the Sacred Congregation for the Eastern Church (May 15th, 1917) and the Papal Institute for Eastern Studies (October 15th, 1917). How, indeed, can the Catholic Churches of the East, which number only nine million faithful, regain their former splendour except by attracting to themselves the large number of dissidents? And what better fruit can we hope for from a deeper understanding of the East, than that of showing the lack of foundation of the schism, and of pointing out the means of reconciliation?

It was under Pius XI that the majority of the conversations of Malines took place (the first one had taken place under Benedict XV from December 6th to 8th, 1921). The private nature of these discussions did not by any means prevent implicit approval from the Holy See. On November 25th, 1922, Cardinal Gasparri wrote to Cardinal Mercier: "The Holy Father approves and encourages your discussions and prays with all his heart that the Lord may bless them." [26]

However there was only one conversation after the death of Cardinal Mercier, the fifth; then Rome decided it would be best to suspend them. In order to call to mind certain essential points of doctrine and discipline which some people were forgetting, Pius XI published the encyclical *Mortalium animos*, [27] in which he shows with apostolic certainty that the only means of reconciliation for Christians is the return of dissidents to the Roman faith and to submission to the successor of Peter. It ends with a new appeal, and asks God, our Lord, to deign to call all the erring back to the unity of the Church. This invocation has been added to the litany of the saints.

Pius XII eased relations between Roman Catholics and other Christians, and was also concerned with dispelling confusion

[26] J. Bivort de la Saudée, *Anglicans et Catholiques* (Paris, 1948), pp. 66–7.
[27] January 6th, 1928, in *AAS*, xx (1928), pp. 5–16.

and indifference. He helped relations between Catholics and non-Catholics by the frequent appeals he made to honest men to unite to combat the forces of evil and to help the unfortunate of every kind whose number has been increased by the war and its results. But he has been careful to see that the rights of truth and the interests of souls should be fully safeguarded. A decree of the Holy Office of 1948, a few weeks before the Assembly of Amsterdam, recalled the discipline of the Church on this point, and forbade any meeting of Catholics with non-Catholics at which, without the authority of the Holy See, religion is discussed, as well as participation in non-Catholic services.

THE INSTRUCTION OF THE HOLY OFFICE

Following on this necessary warning was a larger document which gives the rules for action with regard to the unity of Christians. This was the Instruction published by the Holy See on December 20th, 1949. While maintaining the tenor of the *Monitum*, this explains the doctrine presupposed by Canon Law and points out the conditions for legitimate and useful contacts between Catholics and other Christians.

First of all, we must remove a strange error of interpretation which has been spread by all too large a part of the Press. At a certain point in the Instruction, it says that inter-denominational meetings which are only concerned with safeguarding principles of the natural law and social work do not come into the *Monitum*, and therefore are not included in the prohibition with which the *Monitum* deals in the codified ruling of the Instruction. This point has been mentioned as the main or sole aim of the document, whereas in fact the document merely stated that it was not concerned with such matters. Inter-denominational groups concerned with some definite and non-religious activity have always existed in the past, and they still do exist. One may simply be glad that they are mentioned in such a document, with the simple and obvious proviso that nothing can be accepted which is contrary to the social doctrine of the Church.

The purpose of the Instruction is to give a ruling for relations in interdenominational meetings at which religion is discussed, and at which Catholics discuss on an equal footing with members of other denominations. The Holy See, whose duty it is to permit such meetings, delegates its authority to the bishops for three years. The safeguards and precautions, of which the bishops should be forewarned, are specified at some length. Ecclesiastics should be both able and prudent; laymen cannot be admitted except when they are well instructed and secure in their faith. Large public meetings are not much encouraged. If they are inter-diocesan, national or international the authority of the Holy See is required.

The doctrinal part of the document demands the closest attention. It is founded on the directions already given by the Apostolic See, especially in the encyclicals *Satis cognitum* of Leo XIII, *Mortalium animos* of Pius XI and *Mystici Corporis* of Pius XII. There the Catholic conception of unity is clearly and forcibly inculcated: the only possible unity, the only lawful unity is that of the return of the dissident to the Roman Church. There is no reason to speak of a fullness which the Church lacks and which she will receive with the admission of our separated brethren: rather she will communicate to all who return her own fullness, thus completing the portion of truth and spiritual work which the dissident have retained in varying degrees.

The Instruction requires that meetings and discussions should only be started between Catholics and other Christians when there is a real guarantee of their usefulness. There is nothing cowardly or arrogant in this attitude, but only the maternal care of the Church for the good of her faithful. Not only must the choice of people be carefully made, but also the doctrine of the Church must be declared fully and uncompromisingly in the course of discussions or conversations. Even on the most delicate questions, the doctrine must be upheld in its entirety. Thus the true nature of justification will be openly and clearly stated, the primacy of the Supreme Pontiff, and the Catholic conception of the return of the dissident to the Church of Christ. Thus the two purposes of the Instruction will be achieved, the purity of faith will be preserved, and the danger of indifference avoided. Catholics greatly welcomed the Instruction which they consider to be the Magna Charta of their work for unity.

Non-Catholic Christians, too, should recognize the spirit of faith and charity which inspires this document. Certainly, the claims of the Church are firmly vindicated, every guarantee against doctrinal dangers is most carefully investigated, and the limits for interdenominational contacts prudently fixed. But the Church's care in maintaining her rights and looking after the faithful does not date from today. If there had been contacts between Catholics and non-Catholics under other conditions, they would not have led to anything reliable and lasting, but would only have created harmful illusions, and would have endangered the cause which they were trying to serve. The Church must not be expected to act according to the principles of the Reformation. The Church only asks separated Christians to study, recognize and follow the will of Christ as it is revealed in the sources of revelation. She prays, and urges prayer, so that this work of truth and of grace may be accomplished.

The Church enjoins her priests and her theologians to give, on every occasion, as clearly as possible, competently and charitably, the proofs that the divine will has founded her on the rock and kept her there. She exhorts them to clarify misunderstandings, avoid confusion, and remove the prejudices which prevent so many souls of good will from seeing her true face and recognizing her as a mother. If the conferences, discussions and mixed meetings were not going to serve this end, what would be the purpose in organizing them, or even taking part in them? Do the separated brethren expect anything from us other than a better light on our Catholic faith? The success of such work depends on God and on our co-operation and, before it can be achieved, it will require much effort and certainly many years, but it cannot fail completely if we do not fail in our duty.

The message of Pius XII to Catholics meeting at Magonza should be read, for a complete understanding of the spirit: "We know how deep among your fellow-citizens, Catholic and non-Catholic, is the aspiration towards unity in faith. And who could feel such a desire more keenly than the Vicar of Christ himself? The Church surrounds dissident Christians with sincere love and fervent prayer that they may return to their Mother from whom only God knows how many among them find themselves at a distance through no fault of theirs. If the Church is unyielding with regard to everything that might give even so much as the appearance of an alignment of the Catholic faith with the other confessions or of confusion with dissident Christians, it is because she is convinced that there always has been and always will be but one sure stronghold wherein are safeguarded in a manner infallibly certain all the truth and fullness of the grace which was given to us by Christ, and that in accordance with the express will of her divine founder, this stronghold is none other than the Church herself." [28]

And listen again to the impassioned words with which Pius XII, on the eve of the Holy Year, calls all separated Christians to the great return:

> Oh! that this Holy Year could see also the great return to the one true Church, awaited over the centuries, of so many, who, though believing in Jesus Christ, are for one reason or another separated from her! With unspeakable groans from the Holy Spirit, who lives in the hearts of the good, there rises today as a cry for help the same prayer of the Lord: *ut unum sint.*[29] With good reason are men anxious at the boldness with which united militant atheism is advancing. Now the old question is openly asked: Why still separations? Why still schisms? When will all the forces of spirit and of love be joined in harmony?

If on other occasions an invitation to unity has been sent forth from the Apostolic See, on this occasion all the more do we

[28] *AAS* (1948), 419.
[29] John 17. 11.

repeat it with brotherly concern. We are moved by the pleadings of prayers of numerous believers scattered over the whole earth, who after tragic and painful sufferings, turn their eyes towards the Apostolic See as towards an anchor of salvation for the whole world. For all those who adore Christ—not forgetting those who sincerely but in vain await his coming and adore him as the one promised by the prophets and still to come—do we open the Holy Door. At the same time we offer a welcome from the heart of a father whose fatherhood, in the unfathomable design of God, has come to us from Jesus the Redeemer.[30]

On the occasion of the fifteenth centenary of the Council of Chalcedon, Pius XII, renewing his appeal, referred to the progress of historical objectivity: "Of course We are not unaware that a mass of ancient prejudices persistently hinders the happy realization of the prayer made at the Last Supper to the Eternal Father by Christ Our Lord for His followers: 'That they all may be one.'[31] But We also know that if those who pray, united as in a battle array, are filled with the fervour of a confident faith and a clear conscience, the power of prayer is great enough to pick up a mountain and cast it into the sea.[32] We greatly desire then that all who have at heart this earnest call to embrace Christian unity—let no one who is of Christ esteem this lightly—may pour out prayers and entreaties to God, the Author of order, unity and beauty, that the laudable wishes of all good men may be fulfilled as soon as possible. For attaining this goal, the way is made smooth, certainly, by quiet research, without anger of passion, through which today more than in the past it is usual to reconstruct and ponder events of ages gone by."[33]

Writing to the people of Russia, the Holy Father largely absolved them of blame for the disunity: "Likewise, it is worthwhile to note and to keep in the forefront of our considerations that Isidore, metropolitan of Kiev, subscribed at

[30] *ASS*, XXXII (1950), pp. 126.
[31] John 17. 21.
[32] Cf. Mark 11. 23.
[33] Enc. *Sempiternus Rex*, September 8th, 1951 (*Trans.* Vatican Polyglot Press, Rome, 1951).

the ecumenical council of Florence to the decree solemnly ratifying the union of the Eastern and Western Churches under the authority of the Roman Pontiff and that he subscribed for his entire ecclesiastical province, that is for the whole of the Russian realm; and to this ratification of unity he remained faithful in all things touching him personally until the end of his earthly life.

"And if, in the intervening period—because of a complexus of adverse circumstances on one side or the other—communication became more difficult and as a result more difficult the union of souls (although until 1448 there is no public document that declares your Church separated from the Apostolic See) that, in a general sense at any rate, is not to be attributed to the Slav people and certainly not to our predecessors, who always enfolded those peoples in a paternal love and whenever possible took care to give them their support and to help them in every way."[34]

Again Pius XII writing on the occasion of a centenary to the abbot of the Greek Abbey of Grottaferrata, said: "If all this is considered without prejudice, why should not the biased opinions which have for so long kept innumerable sons away from the bosom of Mother Church, gradually with God's help, yield to the truth? Indeed, the peoples of the East have nothing to fear from re-establishing unity with the Roman Church, or from a much to be desired and necessary return to her; they will lose nothing whatever of the dignity and splendour of their liturgy, or of the revered inheritance of discipline which they have received from their fathers; rather will they enjoy no small increase of strength and glory."[35]

HIS HOLINESS POPE JOHN XXIII

As soon as he was elected Supreme Pontiff and before leaving the Conclave Hall, Pope John XXIII, who had lived for twenty

---

[34] Enc. *Sacro vergente anno*, September 7th, 1952.

[35] *Alacre studium*, English translation in *The Tablet*, August 13th, 1955, and *The Pope Speaks*, II, no. 3, autumn 1955.

years in the countries where the Orthodox are in the majority, showed his desire for the unity of Christians. On January 25th, the last day of the week of prayers for unity, he announced to the College of Cardinals assembled in the Basilica of St Peter-without-the-walls, his decision to convoke an Ecumenical Council. He presented it to the Eminent Cardinals as one of the "certain ancient forms of doctrinal affirmation and of wise arrangements for ecclesiastical discipline. These forms, in the course of Church history, have yielded the richest harvest of results because of their clarity of thought, their compactness of religious unity and their heightened flame of Christian fervour, which we acknowledge (with reference to our temporal welfare, too) as abundant wealth *de rore coeli et de pinguedine terrae* (Gen. 27. 28)."[36]

The announcement made to the public ended with the Holy Father's prayer "for a good beginning, continuation and successful outcome of these proposals ... directed towards light, improvement and joy for all Christian people, towards a renewed invitation to the faithful of the individual religious groups, for them also to follow ... in this seeking after unity and grace, which so many souls, in every part of the world, eagerly desire."

Given the importance of this event, it will be useful to clarify the idea of Ecumenical Council and distinguish its ecumenism from that of the W.C.C., which in French, for instance, is called *Conseil oecuménique des Eglises*.

The Ecumenical Council, as the Catholic Church understands it, is the assembly of all the bishops of the Catholic Church convoked by the Roman Pontiff to consider questions of faith and morals. Its universality in fact consists in the presence of Catholics from all over the world; and its universality of right consists in the fact that the Church has been founded to bring to her bosom all men without exception.

In order that a Council may be called ecumenical, the whole Church must be represented; but that does not mean that every

[36] *Acta Apostolicae Sedis*, 1955, pp. 599–600; English text in *The Pope Speaks*, v, no. 4 (autumn 1959), p. 398.

bishop must be present. It suffices if the chief parts of the Church are represented and in such a way as the pope considers sufficient. Also other people as well as bishops may be invited to the Council and even have a right to vote. The unity of the Council is safeguarded by the union of all with the Roman Pontiff, who convokes the members, and presides over them himself or through his delegates, who must be in agreement to make the decrees of the Council valid. Thus the Council is both one and universal.

Thus defined, the Ecumenical Council has the following characteristics which distinguish it from any other meeting, even a religious one: first of all, its members are conscious that they represent the whole Church; and by this it must be understood that, according to the well-known faith of the Catholic Church, they represent the whole Church of Christ.

Then all the members of the Council have the same faith. They may indeed disagree to start with about the problems which we put before them and uphold their own opinions forcibly, but their faith is such that they are already resolved to accept whatever is decided by the Council and in the way in which it decides.

Finally, the declarations, resolutions and definitions of the Council are imposed on the faithful in the way that the Council determines.

The "Ecumenical Council of Churches", on the other hand, is not a Council at all, but a union of different and autonomous Churches, which remain so, but meet to help each other, to achieve certain ends on which there is agreement, and especially to promote Christian unity. Its spokesmen have no doctrinal authority; they can at most make suggestions, leaving full liberty of decision, to each Church which belongs to it. A general assembly, consisting of the delegates of all the Churches taking part, is convoked every six years. This is an occasion of considerable importance, as has already been seen at Amsterdam and at Evanston. The unity of the Assembly lies in the desire to be together, and in the common belief in the divinity of Christ. In conclusion, some propositions are put to the various Churches taking part, and the thought and religious feelings of the delegates is expressed in a message. Nothing is imposed on the Churches; it is up to them to accept, modify, or to reject the suggestions of the Assembly.

In what sense, then, is the Council and its Assemblies ecumenical? The Council does not by any means claim to represent all Christians, neither does it think that it represents the whole Church of Christ. Many Christians, more than half, do not belong to the Council, and in spite of that, according to the Council's own view, they are part of the Church of Christ. The Council only desires to be universal. It is, above all, inter-denominational, with a spirit of charity towards all Christians and a generous desire to collaborate with them all. Thus there arises a new meaning to the word "ecumenical", which, while it may imply a desire for universality, above all means inter-denominational, and the understanding, sympathy and search for agreement which exists amongst the different sects.

In fact the word "ecumenical" when applied to the Council means above all unity and universality, and therefore authority; while when it is applied to the "Council of Churches" and its work, it means above all the search for unity in interdenominationalism.

Nevertheless, if the Ecumenical Council and the Council which bear the same name are profoundly different, there is nothing to indicate that they are opposed to each other. The Ecumenical Council, by demonstrating and confirming the unity of the Roman Catholic Church, will give an example of unity, and for that reason, as we said in the document announcing the Council, will be an invitation to unity. Further, the clarity and precision which will be brought to doctrine and discipline at the Council, will make a knowledge and understanding of Catholic affairs easier; and that will be an excellent ecumenism in the sense of the word as understood by the Council. At the same time, the Council will give an opportunity to study the causes of disunity more closely, and make known the difficulties which are at present delaying the attainment of the end proclaimed by the Ecumenical Council, namely Christian unity.

CHAPTER V

TENTATIVE APPROACHES

THE OXFORD MOVEMENT

It is certain that the grace of God is constantly urging souls to work for unity of faith among Christians. But there are times when the breath of the Spirit blows more strongly, and when souls áre more attentive to it and more obedient to its impulse. Then, what for centuries has been immobile and seemed fixed for ever, is suddenly roused and goes forward.

One such providential event was the Oxford Movement, which shook the Church of England to its foundations, partly changed it and produced results which still last. Those who are working for unity find an abundant source of light and faith in the study of this great movement. There has been more than one history of the Oxford Movement published; here we offer only a sketch of its principal events.

During the first quarter of the nineteenth century, when the Church of England was growing steadily weaker under the influence of rationalism and State protection, a voice was raised to awaken consciences and to remind everyone of the existence and primacy of the supernatural realities. This was the voice of a tutor of an Oxford College, Henry Newman, who had been brought through a different course to the profession of a doctrinal and living Christianity, which he preached with an eloquence which was efficacious in its simplicity and sincerity. However, he was still very far from the Roman Church, and regarded the Church as the beast of the Apocalypse, when travelling in Italy. A friend of his, John Keble, preached a rousing sermon on July 14th, 1833, on national apostasy occasioned by the suppression of ten Anglican bishoprics in Ireland. A few weeks later, Newman himself wrote his first Tract (September 9th, 1833) which echoes that warning cry, and tries to awaken public opinion. The Oxford Movement had started.

The Tracts followed one another at short intervals for six years; they started as short compositions of four to eleven pages, which denounced the danger of the present state of the Anglican Church and proposed a sort of second Reformation, which would be a *via media* between liberal Protestantism and Roman doctrine. They were not signed, but the first half of them were chiefly by Newman. It is in the second half (from number forty-six) that Pusey appears, a scholarly and profoundly religious man, whose Tracts have the length and importance of short theological treatises.

The first Tracts are still anti-Roman, but the logic of the principles of the *via media* draws them towards Rome. In 1836 Newman recites the Roman Breviary; in 1840 he wants to unite his Church with that of Rome, and many of his disciples are tempted to go further. They must be shown that it is possible to think as a Roman Catholic and yet remain an Anglican. To this end Newman published Tract 90 in February 1841, in which he tries to show that the Thirty-Nine Articles which form the profession of faith of Anglicanism can be interpreted in a Catholic sense. This was the last Tract; in fact it was more than the leaders of the Church of England could tolerate. Condemned by the University and the bishops, Newman drew steadily closer to Rome. In 1842 he left Oxford for Littlemore, where he lived with a few young disciples; and it was there that he preached his last sermon as an Anglican minister in September 1843. Towards the end of 1844, he started to write the *Essay on the Development of Christian Doctrine*. This work convinced him of the lawfulness of the additions which have been made to Catholic doctrine in the course of the centuries. From then on his conscience ruled him. "Life is short and eternity is long", he writes in the moving conclusion of his book. He called to Littlemore Father Dominic Barbieri, an

Italian Passionist, whom Providence had wonderfully prepared for that hour, and on October 9th, 1845, he was admitted to the Roman Church by that holy priest. Several hundred conversions immediately followed Newman's. There would have been many more if all the leaders of the Oxford Movement, and especially Pusey and Keble, had followed their friend at Littlemore; but they were held back till the end, as Newman had been for a long time, by their attachment to a Church which they knew to be sick, but hoped to cure.

Nevertheless, a great change had come about. The return of a part at least of the Church of England to the fold of Peter was now a hope which might be realized in the near future. Since that time, the influence of Catholicism has penetrated into many quarters which were previously hostile.

THE CONVERSATIONS AT MALINES

Background

Fr Jacques de Bivort de la Saudée published in 1949 two volumes of the greatest interest, which call attention to the Conversations at Malines, and explain the setting and results.[1]

The author starts his work with a brief description of the Oxford Movement from which derives the Anglo-Catholic movement which promoted the conversations. From that time, there has been a tendency among many Anglicans to move away from Protestant attitudes towards Catholic doctrines and practices. Various associations were founded by them with the declared intention of working for unity with Rome. Pusey passed on to Lord Halifax the idea that the Church of England was the natural go-between to unite other Christians with Rome. In 1880, Abbé Portal, a Vincentian, met Lord Halifax, and the two men became great friends and worked together for unity, for the remainder of their lives. Above all they were concerned with the question of Anglican Orders. After reconsidering the

---

[1] J. de Bivort de la Saudée, *Anglicans et Catholiques. Le Problème de l'union anglo-romaine 1833–1933* (Paris, 1948); *Documents sur le problème de l'union anglo-romaine 1921–1927* (Paris, 1949).

question Leo XIII[2] declared these orders invalid, thus confirming a great obstacle to unity. But in 1920, at the sixth Lambeth Conference, the Anglican bishops launched an appeal in
favour of unity and even declared themselves "ready to accept
from the authority of the other Churches a sort of commission
or control which would make the ministry of the Anglican
clergy recognized by them" (p. 46).

What was the exact significance of that undertaking?

A memorandum presented by Catholics at one of the conferences of Malines explained it thus: "According to an authorized statement, the first thought of the Anglican bishops was
to clarify their position with regard to the Churches which do
not possess an episcopal hierarchy, the Scottish Presbyterians
for example, Wesleyans, Methodists, etc. The Anglicans would
confer on them episcopal ordination, accepting in return such
form of recognition as seemed necessary for the establishing of
intercommunion among the different Churches for the benefit of
their members. The offer of the Anglican bishops did not, however, exclude the idea of an understanding with those Churches
constituted round an episcopal hierarchy and even seemed to
lead to such an understanding. If all things relating to doctrinal
matters were settled and if agreement was reached on a code of
discipline, there would be no difficulty on the part of the
Anglican bishops in accepting such elements of ordination as
seemed necessary to the Roman Church to place the validity
of their ministry beyond doubt in the eyes of everybody."[3]
Certainly the Lambeth appeal seemed to Lord Halifax an
encouragement towards unity.

Together with Abbé Portal he asked Cardinal Mercier, the
Archbishop of Malines, to organize conferences between representatives of the Roman Church and the Church of England.
There were five meetings which were called the Conversations
at Malines. The first took place from December 6th to 8th,

[2] Apostolic Constitution, *Apostolicae curae*.
[3] Lord Halifax (ed.), *The Conversations at Malines, 1921–1925*,
"Mémoire présenté par les catholiques à la Conference de Malines des
11 et 12 octobre 1926" (London, 1930), p. 299.

1921. On the Catholic side were Cardinal Mercier, his vicar general, Mgr van Roey and Abbé Portal. The Anglicans were Lord Halifax, Dr Robinson, dean of Wells, and Dr Frere, the Anglican bishop of Truro. The Anglicans said that the Thirty-Nine Articles no longer had sufficient authority to prove an obstacle to a closer approach to Rome. They were quite reconciled to the Council of Trent, but more reserved concerning the Vatican Council.[4] Agreement seemed easy on the question of the sacraments, but difficult on that of the pope. The second conference took place on March 14th and 15th, 1923, with the same people. Practical matters were chiefly considered and adaptations which might be made, once dogmatic agreement had been reached. On November 7th and 8th of the same year, the third conversation took place. On the Anglican side there were two new members, Dr Gore, the former Anglican bishop of Oxford, and Dr Kidd, warden of Keble College; while on the Catholic side two members had been added, Mgr Batiffol and Canon Hemmer.

The third and fourth conversations are the most important ones. The chief difficulty of Anglicans, that of the authority of the Roman Pontiff, was discussed. At the third conversation, the Anglican viewpoint was explained by Dr Robinson and Dr Kidd, and Mgr Batiffol replied. They dealt mainly with the position of St Peter according to Scripture and Tradition in the first centuries. The fourth conversation dealt with the pope's relationship with the bishops. Mgr van Roey and Canon Hemmer explained Catholic thought, the former from the dogmatic point of view. Dr Gore compared the Anglican way of thinking with this, and Mgr Batiffol answered him. In 1926 Cardinal Mercier died, and Mgr van Roey succeeded him in the episcopal see of Malines. They decided on a fifth conversation, which was further retarded by the death of Portal in June 1926, and took place on October 11th and 12th, 1926. This was merely a recapitulation of the previous conversations. They agreed to publish two reports, one by Canon Hemmer and the

---

[4] Lord Halifax, *op. cit.*, pp. 11–12.

other by Dr Robinson. In fact, the only publication was that of Lord Halifax in 1928. In June 1927, Pope Pius XI asked Mgr van Roey not to continue the conversations.

The idea

The documents remain and the reading of them is interesting and very instructive. One sees first of all the great difficulty in those conversations, in spite of the good will of all concerned. Four centuries of separation have increased the obstacles, prejudices are deep-seated, habits have been formed, positions have been taken up and must be upheld. Also, the opinions of the Anglicans are infinitely divided. Even among Cardinal Mercier's guests, it is easy to see that, for example, there are important differences between the ideas of Lord Halifax and those of Dr. Gore. The exhortations and letters of Dr Davidson, the Anglican Archbishop of Canterbury, who did not want to compromise "in any way the characteristics and well-founded principles of the Church of England" (p. 82) make any agreement humanly impossible. Yet Dr Davidson had signed the Lambeth appeal.

It was realized, too, that the chief question, as the archbishop himself said, is "the doctrines of the Roman Church concerning the position, jurisdiction and powers of the Holy See".[5] In fact, the Conversations at Malines show a considerable effort on both sides to define their respective positions and to clarify the facts of the problem. The reports of Mgr van Roey, Mgr Batiffol and Canon Hemmer are solid expositions, clear and useful to re-read. How far, then, did they influence their hearers? In the report given at the last conversation, the Catholics maintained that on the question of the special position of the pope in the Church, every possibility of agreement was not to be excluded. They say that the Anglicans "expressed themselves in terms which, while not saying all that Catholics think and believe, yet seemed to justify great hopes".[6]

[5] I, p. 84.
[6] *Conversations de Malines*, p. 301.

According to the same report, the terms used to express the authority conceded to the pope are the following: spiritual responsibility, spiritual power of direction, general superintendence and the caring for the good of the universal Church. The report ends "it transpires from these expressions that there is a feeling for the higher mission of the pope, and that there is a primacy of responsibility as well as a primacy of honour".[7]

The memorandum presented at the third conversation by Dr Robinson on the position of St Peter in the primitive Church is quite significant, as much for what it denies as for what it concedes. He tries first of all to prove that the promises made to Peter were subsequently extended in the same way to all the apostles, and that St Paul, especially, quite independently exercised a certain superiority over Peter. Then he adds:

> Does that mean, then, that what we have already said above exhausts the meaning of the promises made by our Lord to St Peter? Personally, I cannot say that. In conformity with what I believe to be the principle of the "Anglican Church", I cannot accept as final an interpretation of Scripture, which does not take account of that given by the Fathers, or of the providential course of the Church, as witnessed by history. The words "Thou art Peter and upon this rock I shall build my Church" have obsessed the spirit of Christianity and have at least partially caused the dominance of the Church of Rome throughout the centuries.[8]

These words leave the door open for further resolutions and also they contain an idea which might be fruitful, that of understanding Scripture in the light of history. If they were to become convinced that the authority of the pope, as it is acknowledged and realized today in the Catholic Church, is the result of the work of Providence, might they not have to conclude that this result was known, willed and meant by Christ when he said to his apostle: "Thou art Peter and it is upon this rock that I will build my Church", and the rest? It is clear that Jesus instituted what has later been realized by his

[7] *Conversations de Malines*, p. 303.
[8] *Doc.*, p. 95.

Providence. Now, does not everything point to the hand of Providence in the establishment of the pontifical spiritual power? If so many millions of people profess the same faith in the Roman Church in the midst of such different trends of thought, and if a discipline, which is often strict and almost always binding, is accepted if not always observed by the faithful, is not this great blessing of unity due to the watchfulness of a single and infallible visible shepherd? The autocephalous Churches of the East, in spite of their adherence to the first Councils, have within them differing opinions on important points, and above all, they are seriously threatened by Protestant and modernistic infiltrations. As for the sects derived from the Reformation, it is well known that the absence of a visible doctrinal authority has brought them to a state of extreme disunity, and, in many cases, to a great diminution of doctrine. Experience, as history shows, suggests forcibly, therefore, that Providence is to be found on the path which has succeeded, and thus declares itself in favour of the fullest meaning which can be given to *Tu es Petrus*.

Dr. Gore's report seems at first sight to be completely negative and discouraging. Not only does the former Anglican bishop of Oxford declare that he has not "the least desire to submit to Roman authority as an individual",[9] but also his way of conceiving of unity *in corpore* is certainly not acceptable to Catholics. He would like it to be considered sufficient for unity of faith that there should be belief in the dogmas which have always been held, at least in substance by the Church, without any obligation to believe in all the truths taught in the Roman Church as truths of faith. But it is clear that there is not unity of faith when some reject what others believe to be revealed by God. If you refuse to believe in the Immaculate Conception, you have not the same faith as Roman Catholics. Unity requires that all should be bound to adhere to the same dogmas.

Nevertheless, this report leaves the door ajar for a possible agreement. Having distinguished between the fundamental

[9] P. 229.

doctrines which he considers obligatory, and the others, he recognizes that a doctrine can be fundamental and yet only acknowledged implicitly. In such an implicit state it is sufficient for it to be held "in substance". He gives as an example the dogma of the Holy Trinity, implicitly taught by St Paul and St John and made explicit in the third and fourth centuries. But, if it is recognized that a truth can be contained in substance in Holy Scripture or in Tradition without being made explicit there, a principle is allowed which justifies the whole development of doctrine which has taken place in the Roman Church. It is no longer a question of making a distinction between fundamental truths and others. Neither the Councils nor the popes have defined anything as belonging to faith which is not to be found, at least implicitly, in Scripture or the teaching of the Fathers. Catholic theologians have always taken great care to show this, even though they may differ among themselves about the exact way in which it is implicit. Even those who believe that the Church can declare as truths of faith what has been taken from revelation only by means of reasoning properly so-called, such as Father Marin-Sola, usually require that the conclusion should be contained metaphysically in the revealed proposition, which means in fact that it should be present in the virtual state. It is true that a few are satisfied if it is implicit in a wider sense, but all the rest, who are quite numerous, insist that it should be formally implicit.

Thus between Dr Gore and Roman Catholics discussion would turn not so much on the principle, as its applications. And so all hope of understanding is not excluded. Dr Robinson wrote one day: "We distrust logical conclusions *as such*."[10] It is all right to distrust; but only in order to verify, and to submit if the conclusion really is logical.

Agreement, which has not been reached on doctrine, does not, therefore, seem impossible for Anglicans who think in the same way as their brethren at the conversations of Malines. And it is agreement on doctrine which matters. In fact it has

[10] P. 132, note 1.

been established that once agreement can be reached on controversial points, it would be easy to arrange the necessary adaptations for matters of discipline. Certain adaptations proposed by one or other speakers at Malines, such as the extraordinary authority to be accorded to the primate of Canterbury, the marriage of Anglican priests, probably would not be desired either by Catholics or Anglicans. In fact the primate of Canterbury is rather limited, and there are earnest vindications of ecclesiastical celibacy, written by Anglicans.[11] But liturgical or disciplinary customs, which do not harm the purity of dogma, and to which the people were attached, would certainly be kept. Yet it is evident that only rather large groups could claim to enjoy in some measure an exceptional régime within the Church.

Cardinal Mercier, writing to the Archbishop of Canterbury, Dr Davidson, said that the Conversations at Malines had not only drawn hearts closer together, but also helped towards agreement on important questions. That is difficult to refute. Yet it is easy to understand why from the Catholic point of view it was considered best to stop them. The members of the Anglican groups could only speak for themselves; and also they seemed to have reached the limit of what they could concede at present. It was clear that their religious authorities were even less inclined towards an early reconciliation. Also, English Catholics feared that these meetings, which were now known to the public, might create illusions and delay individual conversions.

Perhaps the Conversations at Malines, although called private, were still too official; perhaps they took place at too great intervals; perhaps the secret was not kept for long enough; and perhaps they were concerned too directly with what is called the Church of England, instead of limiting themselves to reconciling the closest groups. Be that as it may, these conversations will go down in history as a generous attempt which

[11] See esp. E. Hawks, *William McGarvey and the Open Pulpit* (Philadelphia, 1935), pp. 192 *et seq.*

has cleared the way of return to Roman unity, and very probably shortened it.

In any case the principle of these conversations has not by any means been condemned. The prescriptions of Canon Law, recalled by the decree of the Holy Office on December 20th, 1949, only require that such conversations should be authorized by the competent authority, which is the Holy See. Also it seems that after the means of prayer and holy example, there is no better than that of discussions, which have been well prepared and which are held in an atmosphere of great loyalty and sincere friendship, that atmosphere in which the noble figures of Lord Halifax and Cardinal Mercier shone so brightly.

CHAPTER VI

THE DIFFICULTIES

Dr Boegner quite rightly spoke at Amsterdam of those terrible illusions which in recent years have followed on some "ecumenical" manifestation in which Catholics, Protestants and Orthodox had talked, prayed and sung together. Then it seemed that unity was almost attained, and indifference in matters of religion was the result. It is also for this reason, if we have been correctly informed, that the Catholic hierarchy in England has had to moderate or even stop certain more or less unionist movements. In fact, true unity, which means unity in a faith which is wholly professed, still presents great difficulties today. It is only by being satisfied with an apparent unity or a limited understanding that one can believe oneself to be near the goal. It is necessary to face the obstacles in the way of unity bravely, because, by knowing them, it is possible to work towards overcoming them.

THE EAST

As regards the East, there is first of all the long duration of the schism which works against unity. Even without counting it from the eleventh century, there are already nine centuries of separation; they are used to being disunited. Catholics and the dissident have each continued in their own spirit, without those mutual influences which used to intervene, in both directions, between East and West. Certainly there have been many attempts at unity, but without the necessary preparation, and without the participation of the people. A great effort is needed today to lift the weight of so many centuries.

In fact separation tended to accentuate the differences. Thus, the Easterns who returned to the Catholic Church also wanted to use the Latin rite. In the East traditional doctrines were called in question as the Church of Rome recommended or defined them.

Such was the case with the Immaculate Conception, and of the eucharistic Consecration effected by the words of Christ and not by the epiclesis.

A lay theologian, Khomiakov, has written many impassioned pages attributing responsibility for the schism to the Church of Rome, and praising the purity of doctrine of the separated East. He urges certain ways of thinking, which are habitual to the Orthodox, so as to make them seem part of all orthodoxy.

His conception of the Church, especially, would reduce the task of the hierarchy to nothing.[1] His influence, which is also to be found among thinkers of an ecumenical tendency, such as Arseniev, blocked the way to unity.

The separation from Rome also helped to bring the Orthodox Church closer to the opponents of Rome, the Protestants. Lutheran and Calvinist infiltrations have penetrated Orthodox theology, especially with regard to the relationship of grace to liberty, and of the natural to the supernatural. The ease with which divorce was granted, so much opposed to the New Testament texts and to the ancient faith, is an important difference of doctrine, and a serious difference in practice.[2]

Also, the Roman Church, like every living organism, grew; and she made explicit what was already implicit in traditional doctrine. She perfected her organization, insisting on the supremacy of the Roman Pontiff, the source, support and guarantee of her unity, while the Eastern Churches, influenced by the nationalist movement of modern times, formed numerous autocephalous groups which had difficulty in maintaining doctrinal agreement.

Then, too, the activity of the civil authorities must be taken

[1] See Manders in *Unitas*, I (1946), n. 2, pp. 33 *et seq.*; n. 3, pp. 33–61.
[2] See M. Jugie, "L'unité chrétienne et la question du divorce dans l'ancienne Église", in *Unitas*, I (1946), pp. 43–61.

into account. In every age and almost everywhere, there are statesmen, or their advisers, who have restricted as far as possible the contact of the citizens of a country with the central religious authority; and who have emphasized the national character of the local Churches. Their activity easily develops in the separated Churches. Those States, which have had control of the bishops and the clergy for centuries, will certainly oppose any step which they might want to take towards reunion with Catholics. Today one can observe the atheistic Communists inciting their subjects to hostility towards Roman unity. Even where there is no dictatorship, the particularist and separatist tendency of nationalism within the State is to be feared. It is necessary to oppose them by resolute public opinion.

There are of course other difficulties, and especially that of the sacrifices required of individuals before arriving at unity, to recognize that one did not possess the whole truth; to admit that others did possess it; perhaps to change certain aspects of one's own conduct; to accept some new dependence and other similiar hardships. In order to overcome all these personal obstacles, a great wave of generosity would be needed, which could only be achieved by a burning desire for unity.

THE PROTESTANTS

On the Protestant side, the difficulties are even greater. Perhaps the greatest difficulty is the disunity which breaks them into so many sects, and does not allow them to be considered together. How can one make up for the lack of an authority which could take a decision and see that it is carried out? While separated Eastern Churches would accept reunion if their leaders decided on it (that at least is what it seems from the present situation), there is nothing to prove that the Protestant sects would follow their leaders, if these decided to go to Rome. Also the leaders themselves are too numerous and too different to take part together in the same movement. As Fr Vincent McNabb, O.P., put it so well: "It is impossible that the Church of Rome should unite with all the Church of England until all the Church of England believes alike."[3]

Then there are the doctrinal difficulties. With certain Anglo-Catholics agreement is almost complete. They even go so far as to accept the infallibility of the pope, without feeling obliged to leave the Church of England. Fr McNabb has also studied the case of these Catholics of desire, and has concluded that: "Yet while it is beyond our competence to see and judge their heart, it is still our duty to insist that no *desire* of doing a difficult duty is, under any circumstances, the *equivalent* of doing our duty."[4]

With others, who are more numerous, and with the rest of the Anglicans, the difference is more pronounced, until it becomes an abyss between those sects who call themselves Christians but deny the divinity of Christ, the foundation of Christianity. Even where belief is the same, or at least very little different, misunderstandings and prejudices have an influence which makes the approach and progress towards unity difficult. For example, the separated Churches have almost everywhere become national Churches, and in some cases have identified themselves with the nation, so that unity seems like a betrayal, or at least a painful wrench. To listen to counsels of unity is in some ways like listening to the call of Abraham: "Go from your country and your kindred and your father's house to the land that I will show you."[5]

A great obstacle is the fact that the Catholic Church does not recognize the validity of Anglican orders. Henry VIII brought about the schism, without adhering to the Reformation, but the Archbishop of Canterbury, Cranmer, introduced Protestant doctrines to the Church of England. In the Book of Common Prayer, the Mass first of all loses its character of a sacrifice (in 1549), and then is simply suppressed (1552). It was in that period (in 1559) that Bishop Parker was consecrated, and he was responsible for all Anglican ordinations. Up till

[3] *The Church and Reunion* (London, Burns Oates, 1937), p. 233.
[4] McNabb, *op. cit.*, p. 230.
[5] Gen. 12. 1.

about the end of the nineteenth century, there was agreement in the Catholic Church on denial of the validity of those ordinations; but because a controversy arose, in about 1890, Leo XIII appointed a commission to study the question and he chose the members of the commission from among those who defended the validity and those who denied it. After receiving the Commission's report, and having considered the matter for several months, Leo XIII published on September 13th, 1896, the Bull *Apostolicae curae* in which he declared Anglican orders invalid. He gave three reasons for this: first, the practice of the Church, then the defectiveness of the rite in which all that designates the priesthood had been suppressed, and finally the presence of an intention contrary to the nature of the sacrament of Holy Orders.

It would therefore be a mistake to think that Leo XIII's decision was based on the absence of porrection of the instruments. Pius XII declared recently that such porrection is not essential. No pronouncement was made about the past, but even if he had extended his declarations to include preceding orders, Leo XIII's reasons would not have been thereby weakened.

Is that decision irrevocable? A few theologians think it is not,[6] but it is difficult not to see all the conditions for an infallible document in the Bull of 1896. However, it is understandable that Anglican ministers feel a repugnance when their orders are called in question. There are some who stay outside the Church for this reason alone.

ECUMENISM AND CONVERSIONS

When Catholics of today are looking for the best way to overcome the obstacles which we have just described, one previous question presents itself to them: Should they join in "ecumenical" work, if only in the specifically Catholic one, and work for the approach *in corpore* of the separated sects,

[6] Cf. *Dictionnaire de théologie catholique*, art. "Ordinations Anglicanes".

or would they not do better to occupy themselves with souls, one by one, and only concern themselves with individual conversions? It is important to consider carefully what relationship of opposition or harmony the "ecumenical" method has with the work of the apostolate which is concerned with individual conversions.

It often happens that isolated non-Catholics ask to be received into the Catholic Church. What is the effect of these individual returns on returns *in corpore*? Are they an obstacle, a help, or an event of little influence?

Many people think that there is incompatibility between individual conversions and "ecumenism". Max Thurian, of the reformed community of Taizé, after recognizing that certain conversions are necessary, adds: "Nevertheless, we should accept such individual cases with sorrow knowing that they create in certain environments (family, friends, parish) obstacles to unity which are difficult to overcome."[7] Thurian carries his idea further still, and holds that corporate reunions are also obstacles to the movement towards unity, such as that of part of the Anglican Church would have been, had the conversations of Malines achieved their end. The departure of some, even in groups, upsets and hardens those who remain. One should rather advance towards unity together and at the same pace. One can read in the life of Newman what fears, what sorrow and what resentment there was among those working for unity when conversions increased in their ranks.[8] Even some of those who recognize the Catholic Church as the true Church are unsympathetic towards individual returns; because they think that the converts immediately lose their influence in the circle from which they come, while if they had stayed there their influence would have continued to be beneficial. And there are even to be found men like Spencer Jones, who urged his co-religionists to recognize the authority of the Church of Rome, and yet thought it right to remain in Anglicanism, in

---

[7] In *Catholicité, Chrétiens devant l'Oecuménisme*, July, 1947, p. 27.
[8] See W. Ward, *The Life of J. H. Cardinal Newman* (London, 1927), especially ch. 3, pp. 79 *et seq.*

which he died at eighty-six. It was *in corpore* that they separated, and so *in corpore* they want to return.

Then there are those who do not believe in "corporate" conversions, that is those made in a body, at all; all their hopes and efforts are directed towards individual conversions, which they regret to see retarded by the illusion of an approaching collective reunion. One of the reasons why English Catholics were on the whole hostile to the conversations at Malines was that they feared that these would decrease the number of individual conversions.[9]

Thus, for opposite reasons, the solicitude for individual conversions was declared incompatible with the work of "reunion". We, however, think that this is an error; but to prove it, we must consider the concrete facts of the problem.

First of all, can one reasonably hope soon for a reunion of all Christians in the unity of the faith? We do not intend to set limits to the power of divine grace, but to judge from what we can observe at present, there is no sign that such a happy event is near at hand. The differences are too deep and too various to disappear in a short time. One can only consider certain bodies separately, and get some idea of what likelihood of reunion there is.

If, for instance, those separated Christians whom Pius XI called "venerable Oriental Christianities",[10] are being considered, the reasons which are in favour of their return to Catholic unity are so pressing that it is not rash to hope for it. The most likely thing is that some of the autocephalous Churches, or at least a few important groups of one Church, will ask to be reunited, without waiting for others to join them.

In that case, it is more of a unity in a body, or corporate, in the sense that the Church which unites remains the same, except for the state of schism. Fr Jugie has recently held that the separated Eastern Churches, recognizing that they cannot

---

[9] See J. de Bivort de la Saudée, *Anglicans et Catholiques* (Paris, Plon, 1949), p. 216.

[10] "Discorso agli Universitari", in *Quaderni Universitari*, IX (Studium, 1932), p. 28.

define anything since the schism, can "without being untrue to themselves" renounce their false ideas, accept Catholic doctrine, and therefore become Catholic as they are.[11]

Protestantism is too divided to be considered as a whole. The same can be said, at least as regards the part with which we are dealing, of all the Christians grouped under the name of Church of England.

It is true that it had been thought that the Church of England might be able to achieve corporate reunion, that is, without giving up its principles. This theory was particularly upheld by Fr Paul Watson, while he was still an Anglican (Episcopalian), the founder of the Octave of prayers for unity, together with his friend Spencer Jones.[12] What these authors in fact said was that, if the Church of England today affirmed its continuity with what it was before the Reformation, why should it not submit to dependence on Rome, as it did before Henry VIII? For his part, Newman had tried to give a Catholic sense to the Thirty-Nine Articles, which, moreover, could be reformed. In fact, the continuity has been broken in many ways, and a return to Rome of all that belongs to the Church of England, including that part which goes hand in hand with modernism, is extremely unlikely.

However, on the whole, there are some sects and groups for whom admission to full Catholic and Roman unity would seem to be the logical conclusion of their recent history.

The Anglo-Catholics, of whom there are about half a million,[13] and a few sects which are still more Roman, whether they know it or not, have started on a road which from Newman on leads to Rome. If they should stop, modernism threatens them. We have already reported above[14] the judgement of the Revd T. Whitton who sees the salvation of the Church of England and of the Anglo-Catholic group only in

[11] M. Jugie, A.A., *Où se trouve le christianisme intégral. Essai de démonstration catholique* (Paris, 1947).

[12] *The Prince of the Apostles* (Graymoor, 1907), pp. x *et seq.*, 222.

[13] This is the figure given by T. Whitton, *The Necessity for the Catholic Reunion* (London, 1933), p. 124.

[14] See p. 39.

unity with the Roman Church. Also, there are groups amongst the Lutherans and Calvinists who are tormented by nostalgia for true unity. The reunion of such groups, which would not be the reunion of a Church, could still be considered as a corporate reunion, that is made in a body.

Faced with such a possibility of reunion which is in some sense corporate, one wonders whether it would not be best to suspend individual conversions. To answer this, it is possible to agree that on the one hand an apostolate which is inspired by wisdom looks to the most universal good and knows, if it be necessary to attain it, how to abstain from any activity which would be less fruitful. This is the choice between two goods, which naturally chooses the greatest good. If, therefore, we found ourselves in the presence of a movement of the whole which offered the possibility of a happy conclusion in a fairly short time, it would be prudent not to try to obtain individual conversions "if these were going to arrest the general movement".

But there are two points to be cleared up. When a soul becomes convinced that the true Church of Christ is solely the Roman Catholic Church, is he justified in not asking to be received into that Church on the grounds that he would be more useful outside it in order to hasten the return of a whole community and a whole sect, or even a whole Church? The answer must be, no. First of all, it is really dishonest to pretend to be still what one is not, and to use that false appearance to influence others. Also, and most important of all, well-ordered charity begins at home. Our soul has been entrusted to us, before the souls of others. We must obey Christ in order to be saved, and one does not obey Christ by staying outside the Church which we know he has founded. This is the same thought which Newman expressed at the end of his *Essay on the Development of Christian Doctrine* in these words: "Time is short, and eternity long."

Then, in case there were conflict between individual conversions and returns made *in corpore,* the doctrine is clear. The apostolate may work for the greater return, but wherever an isolated conversion is ready in whatever way, it may not be postponed.

The other very important question is this: is there really a conflict between individual conversions and corporate conversions, that is, between conversions and ecumenism? We think that there is not. Paul Thureau-Dangin, in his biography of Cardinal Vaughan, writes: "Surely by urging souls to desire unity with Rome and accustoming them to the idea of reconciliation with the pope, conversions are not halted? Even if conversions were stopped in this way, a state of soul would be induced which would later become active. Also experience told him: was it not from among the unionists of the past that so many converts were recruited?"[15]

Also, one should remember that the conversion of any body of Christians presupposes the conversion of each member of that body. Therefore an influence must be exercised of such a kind as to bring about a change in each soul. Such activity is of course accompanied by other influences which are at work in the whole body; yet this activity must be in harmony with the other influences, which cannot replace it, but at most only help its work.

There is also the point of view of right. When dealing with spiritual events, we need only consider the right dispositions, those which come from good will. Take the case of Oxford. Certainly, it is understandable that those working for unity felt sad and tempted towards ill-humour and discouragement when they saw a large number of their comrades-in-arms leaving their ranks to join the Catholic Church. But, on reflection, they should have done as Pusey did, and not renounce anything on the road which they had walked together with those who were separated from them. To be annoyed, to turn back or to join a movement simply because others, who were in it, have taken a step which did not please them, would be to fall from that state of good will, which we should always have

---

[15] Thureau-Dangin, *Le Cardinal Vaughan* (Paris, 1911), p. 82.

when dealing with our own salvation; *Omne quod non est ex fide peccatum est.*[16]

It is true, therefore, that individual conversions should not obstruct movements towards unity.[17] But, can one not go further and maintain that, in fact, instead of stopping them they help them to advance towards their own end? Perhaps the Oxford Movement is an example of it. It is sometimes said that the conversion of Newman arrested it. But has the movement really ceased? What has really ceased, and it is not due to the conversion of Newman, but to the refusal of the Anglican authorities to follow the direction of Tract 90, is the cohesion of a group of men of courage and talent who up till then had fought together; what has ceased, or rather diminished, is the great number and the excitement caused by the conversions. But would there be such a considerable number of Anglo-Catholics if the Oxford Movement had not existed? The movement has changed, if you like, but it may have within it as much hope of unity as it had then.

If we turn to the present situation in the Christian world, should we not co-ordinate our ideas in the following way? The majority of ecumenists recognize that their movement cannot achieve its end without the participation of the Roman Catholic Church. The Lambeth Conferences have stated this explicitly on many occasions; and Fr Florovsky repeated it in August 1948 at Amsterdam: "There can be no real ecumenical co-operation, no real Christian communion and no real reunion of Christians, if Rome is not included". He said the same at Evanston. The same idea is to be found in Spencer Jones' famous book *England and the Holy See*. Catholics know, and so do non-Catholics, that the Church of Rome cannot renounce

[16] Rom. 14. 23.

[17] Cardinal Rampolla thought in the same way when he wrote to Lord Halifax: "It is not true that in Rome only individual conversions are wanted and that corporate reunion is not desired: it is only true that we do not want to obstruct individual conversions, the success of which is closer and easier; meanwhile corporate reunion is being dealt with" (Lord Halifax, *Leo* XIII *and Anglican Orders* (London, 1912), p. 351).

anything which constitutes dogma or morals, and that therefore the only way to include her in reunion is to accept her whole faith. That is why Catholics maintain (and non-Catholics realize that Catholics do maintain it) that the real and true aim of the movement towards unity is the acceptance of the Catholic faith by all Christians. And so, the fact that some reach the goal first cannot prevent the others from continuing along the road.

Let us consider the facts as they are, and from the religious point of view. We have admitted the possibility of a return fairly soon of certain separated groups. As for the others, who are so numerous, one can only speak of a distant hope. More than one leader of the Ecumenical Council postpones the union of all Christians in the same faith till the Last Judgement,[18] but in any case it is likely that unity is a long way off. What reason remains then for suspending individual conversions for the sake of ecumenism?

Can we not rather see the help which these conversions give to true unionism? A conversion causes reflection and encourages the timid; for many it clears the way. When converts are noted for their virtue, their talent, and their position, they attract by their example and can precipitate a wave of conversions. Also those cases of corporate reunion which seem likely to come about sooner cannot but be hastened by conversions *en masse*.[19]

The founder of the religious of the Atonement, Fr Watson, who had for some time hoped for the reunion in a body of the whole of the Church of England, and who later did not expect any corporate reunion except in small groups, still recognized the lawfulness and the importance of individual conversions.[20]

Also we should be the first to ask the Catholic apostolate in its

[18] See *Unitas,* December 1948, p. 254.

[19] Whitton writes that the corporate reunion of Anglo-Catholics, if possible, or at least *en masse*, is "what would touch the conscience of England". *The Necessity for Catholic Reunion*, p. 135. This book explains the necessity for, the difficulties and the means towards such a reunion.

[20] See *The Lamp,* September 1948, p. 331.

work to avoid what could indeed irritate souls. Prudent zeal should make itself acceptable. Nobody can be offended because a Catholic explains his faith calmly and courteously clarifies the points which are contested and points out that the objections and prejudices are unfounded. If an appeal to history is made, we must be scrupulously exact. We are certainly not expected to praise the authors of the separations; but we must speak justly of them. In discussion the more we take care to avoid any air of superiority and any pre-occupation with personal triumph, the clearer it will be that we are only concerned with doing a work of light and charity, and the less resentment and opposition shall we cause.

RENUNCIATION OR ENRICHMENT?

A Catholic has no doubt of the great good which will come to his separated brethren as soon as they come into the bosom of the Roman Church. But may he admit that this will also benefit this same Church?

Is it possible to belong to the Catholic Church, as to the one true Church of Christ, and yet think the return of the dissident will not only bring it a numerical increase but also a spiritual enrichment in the understanding of dogma and the exercise of the virtues? If we answer "yes", we please our separated brethren; we give them a bridge which can be crossed from both sides. Reunion is no longer the unilateral acceptance of Catholic truth, but an exchange of riches, a reciprocal communion until both sides achieve the same fullness. For example, the Lutheran would give to the Catholic a deeper sense of the gratuitous nature of grace, the Calvinist would teach a greater familiarity with the Bible, the Anglican a certain austerity in divine service, the Orthodox a greater experience of the mystical life of the Church. The problem is delicate because we risk disparaging the Church by attributing to her a lack which really only belongs to some of her members.

It cannot, of course, be conceded that on any point of faith, the Lutherans or the Anglicans have a more perfect doctrine than the Catholic Church, with whom our Lord will remain until the consummation of the world. It is true indeed that there are Catholics who are less knowledgeable than they should be about the gratuitousness of grace, or the sanctity of the Bible, or the mystical beauties of the Church. These could certainly admire within the Church wonderful examples of all those aspects which they lack. Nevertheless, these can also learn something useful outside the Church which was not offered to them in their immediate circle.

Let us say, then, that the return of our separated brethren would certainly attract our attention to some spiritual treasures of the Church which we do not use enough, and they themselves would be happy to find them complete, without anaemic diminution, and without deceptive camouflage. And this is a sufficient reason to allow Catholics to speak at the ecumenical conversations, with natural humility, with respect and with charity. It is also sufficient to make the reunion seem not like a renunciation, but rather a strengthening of what they hold dearest, according to Newman's experience, which at the age of eighty-six he expressed in these words:

> What can I say but that those great and burning truths which I learned when a boy from Evangelical teaching, I have found impressed upon my heart with fresh and ever increasing force by the Holy Roman Church? That Church has added to the simple Evangelicalism of my first teachers, but it has obscured, diluted, enfeebled, nothing of it. On the contrary I have found a power, a resource, a comfort, a consolation in our Lord's Divinity and Atonement, in his Real Presence in Communion, in his Divine and Human power, which all good Catholics indeed have, but which Evangelical Christians have but faintly.[21]

Nevertheless, the decisive function of the theologians can be seen. It is true that ideas have not been the only causes of the separation, but without them the schisms would never have begun and would never have lasted. In order to end our disunity, it is necessary to try to understand their main ideas. In

[21] Newman to T. G. Edwards, quoted in W. Ward, *Life and Times of Cardinal Newman*, II, p. 527.

each case, it is essential to understand what Fr Jean Islop, O.P., in an article in *Dieu vivant,* stated about Protestantism: "Our aim, then," he writes, "is not to hide the truth with enthusiasm, nor to batter ourselves against windmills like theological Don Quixotes; but rather to discover the theological roots of the Reformation, in order to clarify the ideas which caused the break in unity."[22]

[22] J. Islop, O.P., "Point de vue catholique sur l'oecuménisme", in *Dieu vivant,* IX, p. 128.

CHAPTER VII

WHAT CAN BE DONE?

The position of Christians, as we have considered it, may be summed up like this. On the one hand, a more universal desire for unity, progress in mutual understanding, a deepening of the requirements of faith, the need to combat widespread irreligion and also some reciprocal steps forward, allow new hopes and make it everyone's duty to work, according to the will of the Master, for the reunion of all who believe in Jesus Christ; on the other hand, there are still obstacles which we have not hidden and which derive from accomplished facts, habits which have been formed, and the necessary intransigence of truth and the opposition of human passions. There is sufficient hope to make the effort a duty; yet too many difficulties to be content with a limited and irresolute effort. The time has come for complete action, in which all the resources of good will should be called upon so that at least gradually the evil of disunity may be overcome. It is not sufficient just to establish and keep up the unionistic organizations and to convoke good "ecumenical" assemblies; but also it is necessary to obtain results with these organizations and assemblies. The end, which should always be kept in view, must be unity in the same faith.

The means are manifold and, let us admit honestly, they are equal to the difficulties.

PRAYER

The first is prayer. This consists of asking the Father through our Lord Jesus Christ, that not only those who are at present united to the successor of Peter, but all those who believe in

the divinity of Christ, may be one. All Christians should pray
that they may find themselves in that unity, ask that it should
be extended to their separated brethren. If the prayer be that
what is certainly God's will may come about, and if it is offered
by all who believe in Jesus Christ, with humility, confidence
and perseverance, how can it not be efficacious?

That was the idea of Paul Watson while still a Protestant,
when he thought of making all Christians pray for unity, and
for that purpose suggested the celebration of an Octave of
prayers to be held between January 18th, formerly the feast of
St Peter's Chair in Rome, and January 25th, the feast of the
Conversion of St Paul.

From that time, the Octave, which is called of Christian
unity, continues to be celebrated by many of our separated
brethren, and since Benedict XV approved and recommended
it, it is also celebrated by Catholics in a great number of
Churches, and often, as in Rome, with great solemnity.

Some Protestants dislike celebrating the Octave because the
intentions formulated by Catholics do not please them. But
Catholics have not all the same list of intentions. Here is a
problem which should not be allowed to become more compli-
cated, but which must be solved while it is still simple.

Clearly all Christians can pray for the general intention. Our
Lord Jesus Christ prayed to his Father that his disciples might
all be one. What Christian, then, cannot make the prayer of his
Master his own, and ask for the unity of all Christ's disciples?
The unity which is asked for is thus clearly defined in itself,
even if the person who is praying does not know how that may
be. It is sufficient to conform to the will of Jesus and pray for
union with the will of Jesus and pray for unity as he desired it.
Once again, all Christians can unite in this prayer, and this
agreement of a great number of Christians, of different confessions, who ask God at the same time to bring them to unity,
is one of the great spiritual events of each year. How can we not
think that it was the Holy Spirit himself who inspired Fr Paul
Watson to suggest this Octave, and that it is he who moves
Christian hearts to celebrate it each year? And how could he

not be ready to grant what he makes us ask for, when the prayer attains to that universality, that fervour and that perseverance, planned by the divinity?

The fact that all are united in the general intentions does not prevent each one from defining more exactly what he believes to be Christ's will, by special intention. It is part of Catholic faith to believe that the unity desired by our Lord Jesus must be realized in the Roman Catholic Church, and that, therefore, those who are outside it should return to it. Therefore, nobody should be offended if Catholics ask for Christian unity according to their belief, asking God to make non-Catholics recognize and accept that unity of faith, worship and government, which constitutes Catholic faith.

The Protestant Oscar Cullmann recognizes this clearly: "If Catholics," he says, "pray as believing Catholics for the unity of the Church, they must pray for our submission to Rome. If we pray for unity, in the way that we conceive of it, we ought to pray that Catholics should cease to be exclusive in the Catholic sense, or in other words that they should cease to be Roman Catholics."[1]

Likewise the Faith and Order Commission when recommending the Octave of Unity in January 1959, said: "Even in our prayer for unity we are divided because of our differences concerning the true meaning of Christian unity."

In fact the intentions which Fr Paul Watson proposed for the days of the Octave, after he had become a Catholic, consisted of asking for the return to the Roman Church of our separated brethren of the East, of the Anglicans, of the Lutherans and other Protestants in Europe, of the Protestants in America, and at the same time the return of lapsed Catholics to the reception of the sacraments, and the conversion of the Jews. Some Catholics, with Abbé Couturier, preferred to choose rather different intentions. They pray for the sanctification of Catholics, Orthodox, Anglicans, Lutherans, Calvinists and other Protestants. These are excellent intentions which are

[1] Oscar Cullmann, *Catholiques et Protestants. Un projet de solidarité chrétienne* (Delachaux et Niestlé, Neufchatel-Paris, 1958), p. 39.

already implied in those of Paul Watson. But they ask for sanctification with unity in view and therefore, because they are Catholics, they know, and firmly believe, that this sanctification will bear fruit for unity, for the return to the Catholic Church of all separated brethren. Really, all Catholics make the same prayer. Non-Catholics should not be suspicious of this. To expect Catholics to pray for a unity which is as yet unknown, would be to ask them to believe as Protestants. Catholics, on the other hand, obviously understand that their dissident brethren make different intentions. After such a long period of separation, it cannot be expected that there should be exactly the same form of unity. The fact that all pray on the same days for the unity desired by the Saviour is already a step towards unity.

The Assembly at Evanston accepted the celebration of the Octave in January. The intentions, which the Faith and Order Commission recommended soon afterwards, are such that Catholics would have no difficulty in making them their own.

The possibility of praying prevents our saying that the end of disunity is impossible. It is because there has been so much prayer that, from so many different parts of the Christian horizon, the desire for unity has been manifested, and the efforts to achieve it are increasing. Normally, God requires our co-operation. When he wants to grant us a gift, he disposes us to receive it.

ACTION

What action should we take, then, to prepare for the grace of reunion? After prayer, the best activity to help towards unity, for Catholics, is undoubtedly wholehearted collaboration with the sanctifying work of the Church. To progress and to help others to progress in the supreme love of the Lord, so that the Bride of Christ may appear as the depository, the inspiration and the guardian of this love, is to create an invincible attraction for souls who are eager for sanctity, or at least concerned with their own salvation. Pope Pius XI thus admonished the apostles of unity.[2] And there is perhaps nothing more moving in all the literature of unity than the prayer of a friend of Newman's, John Dobree Dalgairns, addressed to monks dedicated to the conversion of England:

> May you work among Roman Catholics; that they may show us what we have not, the image of a Church perfect in discipline and customs; that she may be chaste and beautiful as the divine Bride of Christ should be; that she may sing day and night the praises of her Saviour, and that even her exterior vestments may be splendid, so that the spectator may be struck with admiration, may throw himself at her feet, because he sees clearly in her the beloved of the King of Heaven; may you go and preach the Gospel in our great cities to the semi-pagan multitudes; that you may walk barefoot; that you may wear sackcloth; that you may have mortification imprinted on your faces; in fact, that there may be amongst you a saint like the seraph of Assisi, and the heart of England will be won.[3]

It was the reading of this letter which decided Fr Dominic Barberi, the Italian Passionist, to leave for England, and it was into his hands that Newman was to make his abjuration. There have always been saints in the Roman Church as the uninterrupted canonizations testify; but they are certainly needed for contact with our separated brethren; or at least scandals must not hide from the eyes of those whose faith is weak the splendour of the virtues which the Holy Spirit constantly causes to shine among his own. Besides, the thought that we may attract those who are separated from us by a difference of faith is a powerful stimulus for the perfection of our Christian life. Zeal for unity, instead of making Catholics indifferent to good, puts progress in the evangelical spirit foremost: *ut videant opera vestra bona et glorificent Patrem vestrum qui in coelis est.*

This is also the programme of non-Catholic Christians, to achieve unity by means of greater unity with Christ.

By immersing oneself in an atmosphere of prayer, supported

[2] Encyclical, *Ecclesiam Dei*, November 12th, 1923, in *AAS*, p. 579.
[3] Letters to *Univers* April 13th, 1841, reproduced in *Unitas* (French ed.), II (1950), p. 219.

by a really good Christian life, the work for unity cannot fail to be efficacious. What direction will it take? The unity of Christians is certainly a complex question, but it is above all a question of truth. It consists in agreeing about the doctrine which God has revealed, and about the constitution which Christ has given to the Church. It is the duty of Catholics to explain the claims of the Church and her visible head with clarity, serenity, objectivity and charity. Turning to the separated brethren of the East, they must try to show them how the primacy of Rome was recognized by them until the time of the separation and that the Catholic Councils held since that time have only emphasized the idea that tradition had always formed about the successor of Peter. It is necessary to demonstrate the lawfulness of papal supremacy to the followers of the Lutheran and Calvinist Reformation, by insisting on the testimony of the Scriptures, in the Gospel and the Acts of the Apostles. The recent studies of historians make this task easier. The authenticity of the text of St Matthew, which makes Peter the unshakable foundation of the Church, is no longer contested, and the activity of Peter at the beginning of apostolic times is in accordance with such a mission.

A Catholic cannot but rejoice when he sees Protestants keeping and even recently intensifying their attachment to the Bible, for it speaks of the Church of Christ founded on Peter. It is also noteworthy that the idea of Tradition tends to gain favour with Protestants. Cullman shows the authority of Tradition, even before the Gospels were written. And just as Tradition advances through the centuries with the majesty of a river which flows on unhindered and ever widening in its bed, Newman's views on the development and evolution of doctrine make it possible to explain this growth without accusing the Church of having introduced important changes in primitive dogma. Often, it will be sufficient to explain Catholic faith exactly and clearly; suddenly prejudices and misunderstandings disappear. For example Catholics do not believe that the pope never makes a mistake, but only that he does not err when he defines *ex cathedra* a truth concerning faith or morals, with the intention of imposing the belief on the whole Church. In fact that is very rare. When Catholics give to the Blessed Virgin Mary the title of Mother of God, which Origen attributed to her, long before the Council of Ephesus, they do not mean that she generated the divinity, but only that she gave natural birth to the Word, who was incarnate in her. As Mother of Jesus, who is God, how could she not be Mother of God? Certainly it is a high title; but it is so, because of the greatness of God, and consequently to recognize and exalt the privileges of the Mother is to confess and glorify the infinite perfection of the Son. The splendour of the moon gives glory to the sun, and it is the beauty of the moon (*pulchra ut luna*) which the Church celebrates in Mary.

Prayer, example, action, everything then must be concentrated to the reunion of Christians in the unity of faith. This cause is worth every sacrifice. Books and magazines, newspapers and pamphlets, conversations and irenic discussions should continue and increase their widespread help. All who love the unity desired by Jesus, and that ought to be all Christians, should join the societies formed to promote it, and dedicate themselves to it, not only to show good will but with the vigorous and confident purpose of achieving results. The time is ripe. Let men not fail to answer the appeal of Providence!

CHAPTER VIII

THE CHURCH OF JESUS CHRIST

Unity of faith will not be achieved without ardent and sincere theological research. Meetings, reciprocal courtesies and disinterested charity will be an indispensable help, but the intellect must be convinced. Therefore, we think it appropriate to the character of this book to show in this last chapter what the Church of Rome means to Catholics.

The fundamental problem is that of the Church. How can the Church of Jesus Christ be recognized?

First of all, did our Lord found a Church, or rather, did he desire to found, and did he establish an institution entrusted with keeping and spreading his teaching, to serve as an instrument for the work that he would do on earth and to enjoy the graces which he obtained by his redeeming death?

This has been denied in two different ways, by Harnack, who reduces the Gospel merely to the preaching of an interior sentiment, filial and trustful, towards the divine paternity; by Loisy, who leaves in the same Gospel only the announcement of the *parousia,* the glorious return of the Son of Man, and the end of all things. Today there seems to be agreement about rejecting both these systems and reading the Gospel as it is, with the interior transformation which it immediately requires, with the judgement and the glory which is announced for the end of time, and also with the expectation of an indefinite length of time between the ascension and the return of the Son of Man in glory and majesty.

As soon as the text of the New Testament is no longer mutilated according to gratuitous hypotheses transformed into systems, one cannot but see the Church which has been founded and inspired by the loving care of our Saviour. After preparing for her, for a long time, Jesus founded her with all her essential elements and promised her his help until the end of time.

Translating the word used by Jesus Christ, we find in the Gospel the actual word "Church" (*Ecclesia*). At first it was read in the Septuagint to mean the synagogue, but the synagogue with a halo of sanctity, an assembly of the saved, an assembly of the elect. Just as the Jewish people of the Old Testament formed the Church of God, so the people, comprising all nations, whom Christ brings together, will be the Church of Christ: "I will build my Church", and it is really a Church of this world which must fight against the enemy of mankind; "The gates of hell shall not prevail against it."

In fact, it is sufficient to be enlightened by the New Testament, in order to see how Jesus prepares and then establishes the society which was to be the continuation of him, when his presence would no longer be visible, and to see how, from the beginning, the apostles act as heads of the new institution.

From the beginning the Master gathers around himself a sort of nucleus of the Church with his disciples who accompany him at the beginning of his public life.

Very soon he chooses twelve of these; he lives among them, teaches them, trains them and reveals himself to them as the Messiah and as the Son of the living God. He prepares them for the apostolate. He establishes them as his witnesses who must announce his doctrine, testify to his resurrection, work his own miracles, and then unite, under the new law, Jews, Samaritans and all the people of the earth. He who hears them hears their Master, and he who despises them despises him. Whatever they shall bind on earth shall be bound in heaven, and whatever they shall loose on earth shall be loosed in heaven. They are clearly the heads of this Church, before whom the wicked should be brought and should accept their judgement, under pain of being considered publicans and sinners.

But there was one among the twelve, whom Jesus distinguishes from the others, at the time of his public life, at his passion, after the resurrection, and who was distinguished from the others from Pentecost and till the day of his martyrdom and that is Peter. He received everything from the Master, even his name. He was first called Simon, and Jesus gave him the name of *Cephas,* which is translated Peter, and which might be better translated as "Rock". How can one, enlightened by nineteen centuries of history, read the famous text of St Matthew (chapter 16) without seeing foretold there what the Catholic Church has fulfilled? The scene is told as it took place, with that simplicity which characterizes the divine. While they were walking near Caesarea, Jesus suddenly stops and, turning to all his disciples, asks them: "Whom do you say that I am?" It was a real question put to each one. Who, then, is this Master from Nazareth, who has not studied and yet teaches the doctors of law, who speaks as no man has ever spoken and who works the most wonderful miracles out of charity and almost secretly? At least, most people thought, he is one of the great prophets come back to the earth, either John the Baptist, or Isaias or Jeremias or another equally great. The apostles report these different ideas; but now Jesus puts a more direct question to them: "And you, who say you that I am?" They had received all the inspiration and secrets of which the Gospel speaks, and doubtless many others too, which are not found in the Gospel (the Gospels are so short, and the days of Jesus, between two nights of prayer, so long and often so busy!)

The grace which shone forth from the incomparable sanctity of the Master illuminated their souls. Surely, then, each one probably knew the mystery, but kept it in his heart without ever having had occasion to put it into words, until now. Certainly that was so in the case of Peter, and whether he obeyed an impulse of his temperament, or whether he was already in some way the head, it was he who answered: "Thou art the Christ, the Son of the living God."

Thus, this simple man, who had given up his boat and nets for Jesus, knew and proclaimed the great news, the incarnation of the Son of God. "Blessed art thou, Simon son of Jona," Jesus said to him, "it is not flesh and blood, it is my father in heaven that has revealed this to thee." It is this truth which constitutes the Christian, which was foretold in all the figures, which was defended at Nicaea, at Ephesus, at Chalcedon, and at Constantinople, and which constantly resounds under the vaults of the Churches, and which, in our times, non-Catholic Christians have made the basis of the Ecumenical Council at Amsterdam. There lies the glory of the Son of Man, which Jesus, in his discourse after the Last Supper, hails as the essence of his teaching, and as the bond between those who believe in him. So, just as this truth is the foundation of all Christian doctrine, so he who first, by the grace of the Father, confessed it with all his heart, was the foundation of the society which was to continue the work of Jesus: "And I tell thee that thou art Peter, and it is upon this rock that I will build my Church; and the gates of hell shall not prevail against it." Could anything be clearer? "Thou art Peter, and upon this rock. . . ." In Latin, the gender changes (*Tu es Petrus et super hanc petram*) but Aramaic, which was spoken by Jesus, uses the same word, *Cephas*.

The stone or the rock, then, which was to be the foundation of the Church, is not a truth, not even what Peter confessed: it is a person, and that not Christ himself, because he is the founder; it is the chosen apostle, Peter. "Thou art Peter, and upon this rock. . . ." Of course it is true that Peter is the foundation of the Church in that he safeguards the truth and, above all, the principal truth of Christ, the Son of the living God; and also that Peter himself is supported by Christ, the corner-stone on which everything in his Church rests. But what Jesus means chiefly, and beyond a shadow of a doubt, is that all the stones of his Church will rest upon the person of Peter.

At Caesarea, Jesus had spoken in the future: "I will build my Church and I will give you the keys. . . ." This would undoubtedly be enough to prove to us that he had done so. Yet the Gospels show us how the Lord after his resurrection commanded his apostles to continue their mission, and St John, especially, tells how Peter was confirmed in the position which he had been given. Addressing himself again to Simon, son of Jona, Jesus causes him to make up for his triple denial by three declarations of love. And in exchange he entrusts him with all his sheep, great and small, of whom he himself is the Good Shepherd and for whom he has laid down his life. "Feed my lambs, feed my sheep." A truly evangelical scene, in Christ's own manner, which achieved the greatest things with the simplest words and most familiar gestures.

If everything rests on Peter, if Peter is the leader of the whole flock, what will happen when Peter is no longer there? Given that the Church must continue, it must in some way continue to rest on Peter. It is to him in fact that we pray; and it is to his see that people will go. The powers and privileges received on the way to Caesarea pass on to his successors. It is not only today that it is thus interpreted. St Leo in the fifth century declared it formally; in the person of Leo, it is Peter who is considered, "it is he who should be honoured, he who has the watchfulness of all shepherds and the care of all the sheep entrusted to him, he whose dignity is never lost, even in an unworthy successor".[1] And long before that, the Church of Rome declared by words and actions that such was her faith, and quoted the words of Jesus to Peter, "which could not be stronger or clearer if he did mean what Rome says he meant".[2]

Catholic writers have collected many texts, from St Clement of Rome to St Augustine, which show that the primitive Church believed in the permanence of the power of Peter in the Church, and more precisely, the supremacy of the Church of Rome. But, even if there had not been these texts which are so clear and numerous, would it not suffice to consider on the one hand the words of Christ to Simon, son of Jona, and on the other hand what has actually happened in history, in order to conclude that one event explains the other, namely that history reveals the meaning of the divine promise, and this in turn ex-

[1] *Sermo* 2, in anniv.
[2] *A. Maturin, A Memoir with Selected Letters,* by M. Ward (London, 1920), p. 152.

plains history? It has taken some time to realize fully what Jesus had revealed, and it is possible that there will be further developments. But at no stage has reality surpassed what was written. Even today the eminent position held by the successor of Peter (and in fact only one man claims to be that) finds adequate expression in these same words; "upon this rock, I will build my Church. . . ." Whoever reflects carefully on this fact, understands the position taken up by the Anglican Robinson at the Conference of Malines. He admitted that Providence had guided the evolution of papal power. But that was not going far enough. Providence had guided history in this way in order to fulfil the words of Jesus. Christ had history before his eyes when he was speaking to Peter; and he announced what he wanted done. If the development of the papacy is providential, for this reason alone it is difficult to believe that it was not desired by the divine Founder of the Church; but it becomes quite impossible to believe when one realizes that this Founder has said the very words which explain this development, and more so as this development continues. The fulfilment clarifies the prophecy. When I see the successor of Peter ruling over the Church, I am convinced that that is exactly what Jesus Christ meant when he said to Peter: "Upon this rock I will build my Church."

The rest, although it is so powerful, is only the development of those words. Jesus continues thus: "I will give to thee the keys of the kingdom of heaven." Peter will open, and what he opens will be truly open; he will close, and what he closes will be truly closed, just as the owner opens or closes a house. This power of the keys has been interpreted by tradition as that of remitting sins; but for our present purpose it is sufficient that it means the authority conferred on Peter to open (or close) the door to spiritual goods. "Whatever thou shalt bind on earth shall be bound in heaven, and whatever thou shalt loose on earth shall be loosed in heaven." Here, too, the meaning is clear; in this Church of which he is the foundation and of which he possesses the keys, Peter receives the authority to make laws, to judge, to condemn, and to absolve. Do not the words of Christ sound like a formal delegation of his power: You will decide, and how could I withdraw what you have done?

Such are the two aspects of the Church. It is a spiritual society, a society of forgiveness, a society of grace, a society of the love of God and our neighbour. Its own goods are invisible. But it is a society of men, with leaders, and one supreme head, who will remain after Christ has returned to his Father. Therefore, it is a visible society. The parables which Jesus uses to describe the Kingdom of God refer to an external and temporal society, where good and bad are still mixed together. But Jesus had made himself visible in order to bring us the invisible goods. He was the incarnate Word, the Son who had taken human form to enable him to tell men what he had seen in the bosom of the Father. The Church continues him. "The Church", says Bossuet, "is Jesus Christ spread abroad and communicated."[3]

The Church will endure till the end of time, that is, until the return of the Lord, till the day and the hour of the *parousia*. She must continue to be always herself; she must always be the Church of Christ. She teaches the doctrine of Christ, she distributes the goods of Christ, she is constituted as Christ desired her to be, and she has the keys which Christ gave her. If it were not so, the work of Christ would have disappeared. But the work of God never disappears. Jesus is the architect of history and his Church is indefectible. He himself has said so and very forcibly; the powers of hell shall not prevail against his Church. That means that, although he is invisible, he will remain with his own: "Behold I am with you until the consummation of the world." Nobody contends with him; for he has conquered the world. He will send the Spirit to his own to teach them. Here he is dealing with the eternal salvation of souls. "Go teach all nations. He who believes and is baptized shall be saved, and he who does not believe shall be condemned." A teaching which carried with it such serious consequences must have been preserved exactly by Jesus.

[3] *Lettre sur le Mystère de l'Eglise.*

But have we really considered what the preservation of truth implies? It would be foolish to distinguish between indefectibility and infallibility. A society created to transmit divine revelation to us would cease to be indefectible if it could deceive and be deceived. It is not sufficient for truth to be found there only at certain times, or only in part of her members. She should possess it always, and profess it by means of her authorized spokesmen. It is essential to be able to discover where the truth of Christ lies. Otherwise, Christ has not lived on, there is no longer a Church, and no longer any Christianity. And we could perhaps go further still with a writer who repeated what made St Augustine reflect so much on the road to conversion: "It could not be, I thought, that God had provided no place in which the spirit of man might rest. Somewhere there must be certainty."[4] However that may be, if Jesus Christ has founded a Church, he has made it infallible. As guardian of the truth we listen to her. "He who hears you, hears me."

But infallibility requires a spokesman. Undoubtedly all the faithful receive the gift of Christian understanding, which leads them to certain decisions in certain cases, and draws them away from the opposite decision. But this is usually a confused feeling, which can easily acquire disordered elements and which must therefore be controlled, and which cannot anyway resolve every problem which arises. Should the infallible instrument be composed of those who are in charge of the direction of the Church? But to consider them separately, what a miracle of providence would be needed for them all to agree spontaneously about every essential point of doctrine! In fact we can see, throughout the course of history, heads of particular Churches teaching errors, sometimes persisting in them and becoming heresiarchs. Is it then necessary to convoke an assembly which we call a Council and follow its decisions? If, then, the assembly of those who have authority to teach were to profess an error, the Church would not have fulfilled her mission

[4] Stanley B. James, *The Adventures of a Spiritual Tramp* (London and New York, 1926), p. 155.

and in fact would no longer exist. But what difficulties there still are if the Councils represent the supreme instrument of infallibility! When would the Council be sufficiently general? Who would be the judge of its liberty, of its proper functioning, of the majority obtained in each of its decisions, and of the meaning of its definitions? And if one Council which considers itself general opposes another which claims to be the same, who can judge between them? It is essential for the assemblies to have a head, and that there should be only one and that he be able to decide in the last resort. Finally, when one considers the practical difficulties of convoking a general Council and at the same time the urgent necessity that may arise to suppress a dawning heresy or to avoid a threatened schism, one must conclude that whoever has the authority to direct and approve the Councils must also be able to decide, even independently of the Councils, when the faith of the Church is threatened. The personal infallibility of the Head of the Church is a corollary of the indefectibility of the Church. And if the Church requires an infallible Head, who else could he be but the successor of him to whom Jesus said: "Whatever you shall bind on earth, shall be bound in heaven?" Here again the agreement between the needs of the Church and the words of Jesus confirms that we are not making a mistake when we give the full meaning to the evangelical text, and perhaps we should not have done so with so much certainty if the facts of history, such as the needs of the Church, had not clarified them for us.

For its government the Church is a visible society. It is therefore natural that she has visible rites which unite her members and help them in all their needs. In fact we find what was later given the name of sacrament in the words of the New Testament and in the custom of the primitive Church. The mission of the apostles was to baptize all nations in the name of the Father and of the Son and of the Holy Ghost, so that men might be reborn by the power of the water and of the Holy Spirit. They were to renew the mystery which their Master had accomplished at the end of the Last Supper. They were to forgive or retain sins, which clearly implies the existence of a suitable tribunal. There is therefore the union of a sensible action with the spiritual effect. It would be unreasonable to fear that here was a similarity with magical practices. In magic there is no proportion between the cause and the effect achieved. I pierce the heart of my enemy in his portrait and think that I have killed him. The power which I suppose my act has is wholly imaginary. In baptism on the other hand, the power and the mercy of God are at work; the washing which is required only makes the divine action symbolically visible. But it has been objected: is it not interfering with the liberty of the Holy Spirit to claim to make him intervene, or to limit his action by leaving out the agreed rites, by the use of certain gestures and certain formulas? In fact, such a view can only arise from a purely exterior view of things. The Holy Spirit in union with the Father and the Son freely moved the heart of Christ to institute baptism and the other sacraments; freely too he now moves the hearts of men to ask for divine grace through the use of the sacraments; and, finally, it is with full freedom that he moves the minister to act by desiring what the Church desires. It all lies in this, liberty and spirit. And, further, nothing limits the spreading of grace. He who gives it, and who usually gives it through the sacraments, can also, and frequently does, give it without the sacraments. Is it not rather by rejecting the very possibility of the institution of the sacraments that divine liberty is arbitrarily limited?

Understood as it should be, the use of the sacraments by no means deprives one of direct contact with the divine influence, but rather helps it. It shows the condescension with which our heavenly Father treats us according to our nature. "If you had no bodies", says St John Chrysostom, "God would have given you simple and incorporeal gifts, but, because your soul is united to your body, he gives you what is intelligible by means of material things."[5]

A Church which is visible, hierarchical and sacramental: have we then considered all the constitutional features? We

[5] Homily 60, "To the people of Antioch".

must at least add, and this is of capital importance, that the Church is living. Since she is living, she can, and indeed must, move. Far from being surprised to see her developing her doctrine and her customs throughout the centuries, we should recognize in this the wisdom and omnipotence of her Founder. He did not leave an inert society, already beautiful and complete, which very soon would appear strange and ill-suited to the changing conditions of humanity, but a living being whose virtues develop according to a certain order and which make actions which come to her from all parts of the world rebound to her own good.

He who would deny this lawful ability to develop in the Church could not logically stay in any of the societies of today which call themselves Christian. There is not a single one, in fact, which reproduces, without any additions or subtractions, the historical condition of the Church in the first century. Therefore, it is necessary to start by admitting a certain evolution. Newman in the *via media* followed the course of the Church till the fourth or fifth century and thought of stopping there. The heirs of Photius go on till the end of the Seventh Council, in the eighth century, and stop there. But is it not immediately obvious that if the Church could develop according to the will of God until the fifth or until the eighth century, she could equally well develop in the following centuries?

One should not be surprised *a priori* to see in the Catholic Church other features of more recent date, developing primitive features. She is not for that reason different, just as a man is not another person because he is no longer a child. The Church has always been adult, and she will always be young; her movement takes place in the bosom of her maturity. But the movement is real, and moreover, marvellously widespread. Let us cite, for example, the cult of the Virgin Mary, which so many Protestants think they must reject. It is perfectly true that it has become inseparable from Catholic piety, and it is quite possible that there is no church without an altar consecrated to the Blessed Virgin. A large number of cathedrals or important shrines are dedicated to her; Congregations and

Orders bear her name. The "Hail Mary", the Rosary, the Angelus and the *Salve Regina* are prayers which are recited by whoever has not given up praying altogether. Her own doctrine has been enriched. At a certain moment in history an opinion was formulated, which gradually attracted the attention of Christians, which grew clearer and finally became the belief of all. It was recognized that it was contained in revelation, and the Supreme Authority imposed it on the faithful, as an article of faith. And it was thus, for example, with the dogmas of the Immaculate Conception and the Assumption of Mary.

There is an addition there, but nothing completely new. All that Catholics believe about the Blessed Virgin Mary is to be found at least in germ, and implicitly, in what is said of her in the New Testament. She is the mother of Jesus, the Incarnate Word, the Redeemer of mankind. Therefore, she possesses all that is required for such an honour and for such a union with the Saviour. Gradually, the Christian conscience, assisted by the Spirit of God, becomes aware of the riches contained in the mystery of Mary. But it would be a great mistake to think that the exaltation of the mother harms devotion to her Son. On the contrary, it is precisely because a Christian has such an incomparable idea of the Word Incarnate, that he naturally honours the mother and believes that he cannot honour her too highly. It was for the honour of the Lord (*propter honorem Domini*) that St Augustine made an exception of the Blessed Virgin when he held, against Pelagius, that we were incapable of avoiding all sins even venial ones. Experience shows well enough that where the cult of Mary advances the love and homage rendered to Christ are all the more fervent, as for example at Lourdes. Where is the Lord Jesus more greatly adored and served than in the Catholic Church? Where are there a greater number of souls completely consecrated to him and more generous sacrifices offered to him?

In the same progress from the implicit to the explicit, from the seed to the plant, the other additions which have come about in the life of the Church are justified. What could be more natural? If revelation was made, as it was, through words that were heard and inspired writings, it is quite natural that it should develop. When a proposition is presented to human intelligence, a spontaneous reflection takes place which aims at analysing the content in order to understand it better, to compare it with other propositions of the same kind, and from this act there necessarily result arguments and conclusions which constitute a development of the doctrine received and an enrichment of the spirit. The help which Jesus Christ has promised to his Church safeguards the lawfulness and the truth of the new statements.

We must, in truth, admit that to understand the Church, she must be seen with the eyes of faith. Whoever considers her as an ordinary society with the weaknesses, the absurdities and even the mistakes of those who rule her, as well as the sins of those whom they must obey, only sees, as it were, the shadow or the reverse side of the Church. Look rather at the Head, who is Christ, and the soul who is the Holy Spirit. The Church is, as St Paul says, the body of Christ; she continues him as the body continues the head; he gives her life and moves her as the head gives life to, and moves the body. Christ and the Church, that is the complete body. That is the Church, just as Christ established her, with her visibility, with her hierarchy and with her sensible sacraments. One should not think of two Churches, one exterior and juridical, and the other purely spiritual and invisible. It is the same one. She cannot be the bearer of interior graces amongst men, without being in a visible organism. She is, then, all holy, having been entirely formed by Christ. The sinful members which may be found in her do not belong to her because of their sins, but because of what they still retain of hers, that is to say faith and the possibility of rediscovering the warmth of charity. Thus, always pure and immaculate, she is the worthy spouse of Christ, redeemed by the blood of her Spouse. Jesus Christ loves her and will never abandon her. The marriage of Christians is the symbol of this jealous love of Christ for his Church, and that is why it is a sacrament and divorce cannot be allowed. The help promised by Jesus should not be thought of as a distant and general watchfulness, but as the living help of a spouse who is always present and always full of foresight and kindness.

Jesus gives life to the Church through his Spirit. As Son, who owns everything that the Father owns, he, together with the Father, sends the Holy Spirit to his Church. As man, his own soul is full of the Spirit, and he communicates him to his members as befits the perfect Head of a living body. The Holy Spirit is the soul of the Church. Indeed, eternal life, of which we receive the pledge and the first-fruits here on earth, is none other than charity, participation in that love which is the divine life. The love of God cannot be given except by the divinity. Even Christ's humanity can only be the channel or instrument for such a gift. Therefore, all the hierarchy of the Church, and the sacraments, the Virgin and Christ himself as man, are only instruments in the Church which each in its own way helps the direct union of the divinity with souls. Certainly since they are inseparable, the three Persons of the Holy Trinity are together in this communication of themselves; but Scripture and Tradition lead us to attribute it to the Holy Spirit, to "appropriate" it to him, as theologians say, since he himself proceeds from the love of the Father and the Son.

Here, we cannot conceal some surprise. This then is the Church, as she is known to Catholicism, wholly directed towards participation in invisible and divine goods, aspiring through many means to the life of God himself, and receiving this life through the indwelling of the Holy Spirit in souls, living, then, by the Holy Spirit as a body lives by its soul; and yet it is this Church, shining with supernatural light, which our separated brethren all too often see as a purely exterior and juridical institution, a body without a soul! How is it that they do not see that the essence of Catholicism lies precisely in recognizing this real and interior participation in divine goods, this new life, this creation, which has not only been foretold, but actually given here on earth to those who put on Christ? The justice of God and his Christ is not just applied to us without being communicated to us, but it makes us just, that is to say really and truly loving God in all things; not, indeed, through our own strength, which is only the weakness of the sons of the first Adam, but through the strength which the second Adam has communicated to us.

Bride of Christ, living by his Spirit, the Church is the mother of Christians. The Apocalypse represents her, together with the Virgin Mary, while she gives birth and saves the fruit of her womb from the anger of the dragon. In fact, the supernatural life of the faithful is given to them by means of the Church, since Christ founded her to receive and communicate the gifts of his Spirit. Between this mother and her children the same feelings are exchanged as in the bosom of a family. The Church is patient, devoted, and attentive to all the needs of her children. These, for their part, love the Church. To quote first one person, and that a layman, Charles de Montalembert roused the whole French Government, when defending the Church he cried out passionately, "Gentlemen, the Church is a mother!" At St Peter's in Rome the crowds who enthusiastically acclaim the pope when he blesses them, do honour neither to a head nor a king, but they love the Vicar of Christ, the Church at its summit; they love a father.

But we have spoken of the Church without naming those marks which hold such an important place in treatises on the Church: unity, catholicity, sanctity and apostolicity. Our aim has been to describe the Church of Christ as she is, rather than to distinguish her from what she is not. Alas, we should agree that, today, at least a great number of our separated brethren recognize that the Church ought to be one, and that they do not possess that unity. But in spite of that, they think they belong to the Church, which, according to them, is not the Catholic Church, but the assembly of Christians who have lost unity, and are searching for it, but who may not find it until the end of time, or in heaven. It seems as though they speak like this only because they will not give the full meaning to the indefectibility of the Church, which, as we have seen, is guaranteed by the words of the Lord himself in Holy Scripture. That means that the power and the wisdom of Christ are called in question. He founded only one Church; he wanted this Church to be truly one so that she might declare the same truth; and he solemnly asked his Father for this unity.

Is it possible that he was not heard? Is it really possible that what he desired, established, and promised to help for all time, could not withstand the usury of time and the malice of men? Did he, then, not know how to make a lasting work? Or was he not able to maintain her, he, to whom all power in heaven and on earth has been given? And if, indeed, there does exist today on this earth a Church which is truly one, in which all the members profess the same faith because they recognize the same supreme authority, is it not obvious that this authority has been established by the wisdom of Christ and maintained through the vicissitudes of history by his divine power?

Catholicity is related to unity. One can, in the abstract, call the collection of the denominations which bear the name of Christian a universal Church; but clearly this is a trick of logic which contradicts the truth. One could just as well call all the soldiers of the world a universal army. It is one united Church which should be universal.

The same can be said of apostolicity, which means unity throughout the ages. Wherever there has been a break in the transmission of powers; wherever doctrine has been, not developed and explained, but changed or suppressed, the link with the Church of the apostles has been broken; and it is a different religious society which has appeared.

The Church of Christ cannot but be holy, since her Head is Jesus and her soul the Holy Spirit. She has been abundantly assured that the divine influence will give life to her members and that the Christian virtues will shine forth. Here it suffices to say that, on the one hand, the Church which claims to be the only Church of Christ should show sanctity in a higher degree than the other Christian societies, and that, on the other hand, every religious sect which advances in the practice of the virtues naturally tends towards the unity desired by Christ.

At the end of our reflections, it seems as though we ought to reach a conclusion, which we would like everyone else who is interested in ecumenical problems to consider. The Church of Christ cannot have disappeared. She is still on the earth. Jesus desired this Church to be hierarchical and united. Therefore she does not consist in that multitude of societies which all call themselves Christian, yet are independent of each other, sometimes hostile, and which differ on essential questions of faith. Only one of these societies is the Church of Christ. If this did not exist, the Incarnate Word would have failed in his work, and it would be useless to hope for Christian unity. Undoubtedly, it would be possible to arrive at an agreement amongst all the Christian confessions on a minimum which would be acceptable to all. But a gathering thus obtained would be a human work, the lawfulness of which no authority could guarantee, and which, in any case, would certainly not be the Church founded by Christ, one, hierarchical and indefectible. The only hope, therefore, for Christian unity lies in the actual existence of a Christian society, which possesses unity of faith, government and worship, and in the possibility of the other Christian societies coming to this same faith, under this same government and this same worship. Those who claim that this belief, by which the Catholic Church professes that she alone is the Church of Christ, is an obstacle to Christian unity are certainly mistaken. Far from being an obstacle, this faith is the indispensable condition for the achievement some day of Christian unity.

THE SECOND VATICAN COUNCIL

THE COUNCIL'S PURPOSE

Because in first announcing the Council the Pope spoke of it as a means of helping towards the reconciliation of those Christians at present separated from the Apostolic See many people imagined that the Council would be an actual Council for union, that is, a Council at which means would be sought to reach an understanding with the dissident Eastern Churches and perhaps even with the Protestants. This was an obvious mistake since the requisite conditions for such a Council, like those of Lyons and Florence, at which the union with the Greeks was announced, are far from being realized. For this it would be necessary that all should be convinced already of the necessity for union with the Catholic Church and that the only question needing discussion should be the way in which this could be achieved. We have not yet reached this point. Within a short space of time other, more explicit announcements dispelled all illusion on this point. In his first Encyclical, *Ad Petri cathedram*, the Pope set down very clearly the aims of the Council:

> The principal aim of the Council is to promote the interests of the Catholic faith and a salutary moral renewal among Christian people and to bring ecclesiastical discipline up to date according to the needs of the time. There is no doubt that this will constitute a wonderful spectacle of truth, unity and charity which,

observed by those who are separated from this Apostolic See, will act as a certain invitation to them, we hope, to seek and return to that unity for which Jesus Christ prayed so fervently to his Father.

Essentially, the Council is for the Roman Catholic Church, but the greater splendour given thereby to her unity and holiness will provoke, the Pope trusts, thoughts of union among our separated brethren.

THE SECRETARIAT FOR THE UNION OF CHRISTIANS

By his *motu proprio* of June 5th, 1960 (*Superno Dei nutu*) the Pope, taking into consideration the conclusions of a preparatory commission, organized the preparation of the Council by setting up ten preparatory commissions, two secretariats (a third was later established) and a central commission under his own presidency. One of the secretariats had for its object the union of Christians and it was announced in these terms:

> To show also our love and goodwill towards those who bear the name of Christian, but are separated from this Apostolic See, and in order that they too may be able to follow the labours of the Council and more easily find the way which leads to that unity for which Jesus Christ prayed so fervently to his Father, we institute a special committee or secretariat, under the presidency of a cardinal chosen by us, and organized on the same pattern as the commissions.

The cardinal chosen was Cardinal Bea, a German Jesuit, for long rector of the Biblical Institute and in close touch with ecumenical questions. He defined the secretariat's work as follows:

> In order that the secretariat may be able to act on a sound basis it needs first and foremost information about the ecumenical situation of the different countries in everything concerning questions of union and relations between Catholics and separated brethren, together with those events and facts

which can assist or impede the activity of the secretariat. We shall be grateful for all information sent to us, for all suggestions, for advice and also for criticism. Work in so vast and so varied a field can only be fruitfully carried out with the unprejudiced and constructive collaboration of all those who are competent in this field. In other words we shall accept suggestions made to us on doctrinal, liturgical, ascetical, disciplinary and juridical questions as also on practical questions for the purpose of formulating concrete proposals which can be addressed to the Council or the Roman Curia. With the help of its members and consultors the Secretariat will do its utmost to examine all matters calmly and diligently and then to formulate concrete proposals to put before the central commission (quoted in *Civiltà Cattolica*, 1961, II, p. 73).

THE ARCHBISHOP OF CANTERBURY'S VISIT TO THE POPE

Pope John XXIII's efforts in convening the Council and setting up the secretariat were generally welcomed by Christians separated from Rome, Orthodox, Anglicans and Protestants, and were the cause or at least influenced certain of their recent activities. Journeys were undertaken during 1959 by the patriarchs of Serbia, Antioch, Jerusalem, Alexandria and by the archbishop of Athens in order to take counsel together. But the journey which created a sensation was that made by the patriarch of Constantinople in November and December of the same year. It was known that His Holiness Athenagoras had from the outset shown himself favourably inclined to Pope John XXIII's first acts. It was known, too, that he had in mind a council of Churches wider in scope than that of Geneva which would not be concerned with doctrinal questions and would be able to include the Roman Church. This was not to be the final aim but a first stage enabling further progress to be made. The patriarch travelled to Syria and then to Jerusalem. He made the following statement to a journalist: "I am taking advantage of this pilgrimage to call on all the religious leaders of the Christian communities to collaborate in working for the union of the two Churches, Orthodox and Catholic. I invite all the members of the clergy of this city to work for the realization of this union, especially here where our Lord called us all to love, peace and unity." The patriarch then went to Alexandria, Cairo and Beirut and began to speak of a panorthodox meeting on the island of Rhodes. Next the patriarch of Moscow, Alexis, took up the pilgrim's staff and visited the same Churches as the ecumenical patriarch Athenagoras. He even went to Constantinople and was present at the Christmas liturgy in the Patriarchal Church. He, too, spoke of union among the Orthodox Churches, but he understood it in a sense hostile to Rome. In Greece, he was reminded in no uncertain terms that in the Orthodox Church the primacy belonged to the patriarch of Constantinople.

The Eastern Churches also received a visit from another Church leader, the Anglican archbishop of Canterbury. Everywhere he spoke of unity and peace. But what made his journey one of special importance was his entirely personal decision to conclude it in Rome by a visit to John XXIII. He declared his intention of doing so several weeks in advance. The visit took place on December 2nd, 1960. It was an historic event which cannot fail to have successful results.

Of course, these results should not be overestimated. No *rapprochement* in matters of faith between the two representatives could be expected. As the Pope himself stated, the conversation did not go beyond the threshold of the serious questions separating the Anglican communion and the Roman Church. For his part, the archbishop constantly made it clear that this was a courtesy visit, a matter of Christian charity. It would be a mistake to think that between Anglicans and Catholics the mountains have been made low and the valleys filled in and that henceforward differences can be disregarded. This visit left theological problems exactly as they were.

The importance of this event lies elsewhere. The Anglican archbishop desired to acknowledge the Holy Father's moving attempt to establish among all Christians an atmosphere of confidence and sympathy, and by that very fact he lent his support to the Pope's action with a courage that must have struck those Churches which are members of the World Council of Churches.

Dr Fisher's was a Christian gesture which, after four hundred years of separation, required real wisdom and decision. It was both evidence and, to some extent, the cause, of a new attitude on the part of Anglicans towards the papacy; in fact, general opinion in England, with few exceptions, was in favour of the visit. The House of Lords in the British parliament discussed the matter very sympathetically (*Official Report*, May 10th, 1961).

THE RHODES CONFERENCE

The panorthodox conference planned by the patriarch of Constantinople took place at Rhodes between September 24th and October 1st, 1961. Taking part were twelve Churches, among which were included all the great patriarchates. The purpose of the conference was limited to drawing up an agenda for a future prosynod. The importance of the event lies in the fact that such a conference could take place. Patriarch Athenagoras' prestige was thereby greatly increased.

A well-known Greek theologian, M. Alivisatos, hailed the event in the following terms:

The Rhodes interorthodox conference has now been held after the many hesitations and postponements due to the irresponsible action of certain ecclesiastics and layfolk. For the first time for centuries, under the aegis of the first patriarchate of the whole Orthodox Church, representatives of all the Orthodox Churches, united among themselves by the same faith and the same tradition, have met together. In the foreign atmosphere of the modern world, for the first time for centuries, the various branches of the Orthodox Church have enjoyed the opportunity to see to what extent they are able to agree among themselves and at the same time to evolve and show forth clearly and with dignity a common consciousness of their orthodoxy before the whole of Christendom (*Apostolos Andreas*, September 27th, 1961).

Mgr Iakovos, the metropolitan of Philadelphia and head of the Orthodox Churches of Greek rite in North and South America, has thus summed up the results of the conference:

> If the Rhodes conference was a courageous and audacious gesture the prospects that it has revealed will require considerably more daring, together with self-confidence and hard work; some time will be necessary for an exhaustive study of a great many problems. Already the meeting together in the same place, prayer offered in common around Christ's table of love and team-work under the action of the Holy Spirit have been a stimulus to consciences and a proof of the usefulness of the conference both for the present and the future of Orthodoxy. In addition, the presence of foreign observers must have renewed in them a nostalgia for unity, encouraged by the democratic spirit and conciliar system of Orthodoxy. For all these reasons the prospects revealed by the Rhodes conference seem bright and fruitful for the Christian world (*Apostolos Andreas*, October 4th, 1961; cf. *Unitas*, French edn, 1961, p. 123).

THE NEW DELHI ASSEMBLY

The third Assembly of the World Council of Churches took place in New Delhi, the capital of India, from November 18th to December 6th, 1961. Important resolutions were passed; they had been prepared at the meetings of the Central Committee, especially at that held at St Andrews in 1960. In the first place, the Basis, or confession of faith, required for admission to the Council, was modified. Hitherto the formula required acceptance of "our Lord Jesus Christ as God and Saviour". It has now been completed by explicit mention of the divine Trinity as follows: "The World Council of Churches is a fellowship of Churches which accept our Lord Jesus Christ as God and Saviour, according to the Scriptures, and which strive to correspond with their common vocation for the glory of the one God, Father, Son and Holy Spirit."

The Assembly approved the admission to the Council of twenty-three member Churches, among which were included the Church of Moscow. As a result, the Orthodox, while remaining a small minority, became a real force in the Council. As usual, the Orthodox at Delhi firmly maintained their traditional positions.

The Assembly approved the integration of the International Missionary Council, an association of several Protestant Missionary societies, with the World Council. The Orthodox who were at first opposed to this association finally agreed to it. The members of the World Council desired in this way to encourage evangelization but also to introduce into the missions the ecumenical spirit. Catholics cannot fail to experience some apprehension at this fusion which will help the progress of Protestantism, widen divisions still further and render the task of Catholic missions more difficult.

A decision taken at New Delhi, and which seems to constitute a real step forward, is the proposal to member Churches of a more definite statement of unity, though despite its already complex nature it will probably have to be completed, particularly by inclusion of an authority capable of fulfilling the conditions. In its present form it is the expression of an auspicious ideal for ecumenical work.

For some time past the Faith and Order Commission has given evidence of a certain discontent at the place assigned to it in the Council. In fact, it represents one of the two movements (the other is Life and Work) whose amalgamation constituted the World Council. Yet it has only the rank of a commission in one of the divisions of the Council. Thus it objected that its own aim, theological work for the fostering of unity in faith, was not sufficiently prominent in the Council's work and it called for more attention to be paid to this. At Delhi this demand was to some extent satisfied. Faith and Order remains a simple commission but has been enlarged; it is now composed of 120 members with a budget in proportion at its disposal.

In addition it should be noticed that the Delhi Assembly was the first to receive officially appointed Catholic observers.

CONVOCATION OF THE COUNCIL

For the past three years intensive preparatory work for the coming Council has been going on in Rome and throughout the world. John XXIII, judging that this work was nearing completion, published the Bull convoking the Council on Christmas day, 1961. After showing how the time was ripe for a new General Council he went on:

"At a time ... when generous and increasing efforts are being made in various places for the purpose of restoring the visible unity of all Christians, according to our divine Redeemer's desire, it is natural that the coming Council should provide those basic clarifications of doctrine and mutual charity which will arouse among our separated brethren the desire for the return to unity while at the same time smoothing the way for it.

"[Convocation of the Council:] Therefore, having taken the advice of our brethren the cardinals of the Holy Roman Church, under the authority of our Lord Jesus Christ, of the holy apostles Peter and Paul and of our own we fix, announce and convoke for this year of 1962 the general Ecumenical Council which will be held in the Vatican basilica on days to be fixed according to the opportunity that Providence makes known to us. [The Pope summons the faithful to prayer and adds:] We also invite all Christians belonging to Churches separated from Rome to take part in this chorus of prayer, for the Council will desire to benefit them as well. We know that there are many among them who yearn to return to unity and peace in accordance with Christ's teaching and prayer. We know, too, that the announcement of the Council has not only been gladly welcomed by them but that very many have promised to offer their prayers for its success and hope to send representatives of their communities to follow its labours. All this gives us great comfort and hope and it is especially to facilitate these contacts that we have instituted a Secretariat for this purpose."

SELECT BIBLIOGRAPHY

In this series: DVORNIK, Francis: *The General Councils of the Church*; TAVARD, George: *Protestantism*.

ANSON, Peter F.: *The Benedictines of Caldey*, London, Burns and Oates, 1940.

BAUM, Gregory: *That They May Be One: A Study of Papal Documents (Leo XIII–Pius XIII)*, London, Bloomsbury Publishing Co., 1958.

BELL, G. K. A. (Editor): *Documents of Christian Unity*, three series, London and New York, Oxford Univ. Press, 1924, 1930, 1949.

BOSSUET, Jacques Bénigne: *Variations of the Protestant Churches*, New York, Kenedy, 1902.

BRANDRETH, H. R. T.: *Unity and Reunion: A Bibliography*, London, Black, 1948; *The Œcumenical Ideals of the Oxford Movement*, London, S.P.C.K., 1947.

BROWN, William Adams: *Towards a United Church*, New York, Scribners, 1946.

BULGAKOV, Sergius: *The Orthodox Church*, translated by G. S. Cram, London, Centenary Press, 1935.

CHESTERTON, G. K.: *The Catholic Church and Conversion*, New York, Macmillan, 1929, London, Burns and Oates, 1960.

CONGAR, M. J., O.P.: *Divided Christendom*, London, Geoffrey Bles, and Westminster, Md, Newman Press, 1939.

DUMONT, C. J., O.P.: *Approaches to Christian Unity*, London, Darton, Longman and Todd, 1959.

DUN, Angus: *Prospecting for a United Church*, New York, Harper, 1948.

DVORNIK, Francis: *The Photian Schism: History and Legend*, Cambridge and New York, Cambridge Univ. Press, 1948.

FORTESCUE, Adrian: *The Orthodox Eastern Church*, London, Catholic Truth Society, 1929.

GRISAR, Hartmann: *Martin Luther, His Life and Work*, Westminster, Md, Newman Press, 1950.

HALIFAX, Lord: *The Conversations at Malines 1921–5, Original Documents*, London, Philip Alan, 1930; *Reunion and the Roman Primacy*, New York, Morehouse, 1925; *Notes on the Conversations at Malines, 1921–5*, New York, Morehouse, 1925.

HORTON, Walter M.: *Towards a Reborn Church*, New York, Harper, 1949; *Christian Theology: An Ecumenical Approach*, New York, Harper, 1955.

HOUFE, Ruth, and NEILL, S. C.: *A History of the Ecumenical Movement, 1917–48*, London, S.P.C.K., 1954.

IREMONGER, F. A.: *William Temple, Archbishop of Canterbury*, London and New York, Oxford Univ. Press, 1953.

JONES, Spencer: *Rome and Reunion*, London and New York, Longmans, 1904.

KELLER, Adolph: *Christian Europe Today*, New York, Harpers, 1942.

MANNING, Cardinal H. E.: *England and Christendom*, London, Longmans, 1867.

MCNABB, Vincent, O.P.: *The Church and Reunion*, London, Burns and Oates, 1934.

NEWMAN, Cardinal J. H.: *Apologia pro vita sua*, London, Longmans, 1931, and New York, Doubleday (Image Books); *Certain Difficulties Felt by Anglicans in Catholic Teaching*, two volumes, London, Longmans, 1897.

SLOSSER, Gaius J.: *Christian Unity, Its History and Challenge*, New York, Dutton, 1929.

SODERBLOM, Nathan: *Christian Fellowship or the United Life and Work of Christendom*, New York, Revell, 1923.

ST JOHN, Henry, O.P.: *Essays in Christian Unity*, London, Blackfriars, and Westminster, Md, Newman Press, 1955.

TAVARD, George H.: *The Catholic Approach to Protestantism*, New York, Harper, 1955; *Holy Writ or Holy Church: The Crisis of the Protestant Reformation*, London, Burns and Oates, and New York, Harper, 1959; *Two Centuries of Ecumenism*, London, Burns and Oates, and Chicago, Fides, 1961.

TODD, John M.: *Catholicism and the Ecumenical Movement*, London and New York, Longmans, 1956.

VAN DER POL, W. H.: *The Christian Dilemma*, London, Allen, and New York, Philosophical Library, 1957.

WAND, J. W. C.: *The Church, Its Nature, Structure and Function*, New York, Morehouse, 1948; *What the Church of England Stands For*, London, Mowbray, and New York, Morehouse, 1951; *The Anglican Communion, A Survey*, London and New York, Oxford Univ. Press, 1948.

WARD, Wilfrid: *Life and Times of Cardinal Wiseman*, two volumes, London, Longmans, 1897; *Life of John Henry, Cardinal Newman*, two volumes, London, Longmans, 1913.

WATSON, Paul James Francis, and JONES, Spencer: *The Prince of the Apostles*, Peekshill, New York, Lamp Publishing Co., 1907.

WEIGEL, Gustave, S.J.: *A Catholic Primer on the Ecumenical Movement*, Westminster, Md, Newman Press, 1957; *A Survey of Protestant Theology in Our Day*, Westminster, Md, Newman Press, 1954.

WHITTON, T.: *The Necessity for Catholic Reunion*, London, Williams and Norgate, 1933.

The Twentieth Century Encyclopedia of Catholicism

The number of each volume indicates its place in the over-all series and not the order of publication.

All titles are subject to change.